Tales from
the
Western Front

Ed Dixon

*To Duncan &
Maureen with best
wishes.
Ed*

TALES FROM THE WESTERN FRONT

An Account of my Ramblings in Flanders and France

Ed Dixon

Tales from the Western Front by Ed Dixon.

First published in Great Britain in 2017 by Extremis Publishing Ltd.,
Suite 218, Castle House, 1 Baker Street, Stirling, FK8 1AL, United Kingdom.
www.extremispublishing.com

Extremis Publishing is a Private Limited Company registered in Scotland
(SC509983) whose Registered Office is Suite 218, Castle House, 1 Baker Street,
Stirling, FK8 1AL, United Kingdom.

A CIP catalogue record for this book is available from the British Library.

ISBN: 978-0-9934932-8-7

Typeset in Goudy Bookletter 1911, designed by The League of Moveable Type.

Printed and bound in Great Britain by IngramSpark, Chapter House, Pitfield, Kiln
Farm, Milton Keynes, MK11 3LW, United Kingdom.

Cover artwork is Copyright © Wickerwood at Shutterstock.
Cover design and book design is Copyright © Thomas A. Christie.
Author image is Copyright © Janey Dixon.
Chapter heading illustrations are Copyright © Mohamed Ibrahim at Clker.com.

While every reasonable effort has been made to contact copyright holders and
secure permission for all images reproduced in this work, we offer apologies for
any instances in which this was not possible and for any inadvertent omissions.

**For Janie,
Lynn & Katie**

CONTENTS

TALES FROM THE WESTERN FRONT

An Account of my Ramblings in Flanders and France

Ed Dixon

INTRODUCTION

What you are about to read is not intended to be a guidebook to the battlefields of the Great War, nor a military history in the traditional sense. Instead, in the time-honoured way, I'm going to tell you a story, during the course of which we'll meet up with a cast of characters both living and dead who have given me a lot of laughs, an occasional tear and a truck load of memories. Hopefully you'll find these men and women as interesting and amusing as I have done. So turn on the engine, it's time to be off on a great adventure.

CHAPTER 1

ON THE ROAD AGAIN

FOR me, living as I do in Central Scotland many miles from Eurotunnel or the Channel ports, the most convenient crossing to the Continent is over the old German Ocean from Hull to Zeebrugge via P&O North Sea Ferries. It's always a thrill to drive down through the borderlands of Scotland and England and across the moors of Cumbria to the old cattle drovers' rendezvous at Scotch Corner. From there it's down the A1 past Catterick Camp where the sign for the Marne Barracks reminds me of what lies ahead. Arriving in Hull some six hours and three hundred miles later I join the queue of vehicles waiting on the quayside at the King George VI Dock in the shadow of the gleaming blue and white liveried ferry.

For me, the voyage to Zeebrugge isn't just a means of getting there; it's also a most pleasurable part of the trip. To gaze out from the comfort of the lounge on the upper deck while the pianist conjures up pleasant memories in the tinkle of familiar tunes seems not just a pleasure but almost a privilege. Little villages and farms slip by as the ship glides over the murky waters of the Humber, out past Spurn Head and into the usually grey North Sea. The lights from isolated homesteads make me wonder what the occupants are doing as we pass. Once I saw a football match in progress at a tiny hamlet where the players and spectators must have outnumbered the inhabitants of the houses. It was a scene which could have taken place at any time, maybe even in that glorious summer of 1914 just before the unsuspecting British public was engulfed in war.

Next morning, it's down to the Four Seasons Restaurant for the almost mandatory "Full English" breakfast. Afterwards I spend my remaining time on board watching from my cabin window until I see the white monoliths that are the hotels of Blankenberg looming ever nearer. Then the Mole at Zeebrugge, site of the actions on St George's Day, 1918, comes into view and it's time to get down to the car. After passport control I'm on the road once more and passing the massive redbrick stump of the church at Lissewege, a sight which somehow establishes for me that I'm once again in Flanders and the game, as Sherlock would have it, is quite definitely afoot. It was only recently after many years of by-passing it that I finally drove down to the little village and found, much to my surprise, that there, nestling close to the cranes, railways and docks of Zeebrugge, was a whitewashed haven of peace, well worth the slight detour.

My usual itinerary is first to visit the Somme in France and then drive back up the road to Ypres in Belgium. There's a kind of dramatic, emotional logic to this sequence which I hope will become more obvious as my journey progresses. The drive south is usually quite straightforward, if a little hectic, due to the volume of traffic coming from the coast and elsewhere bound for Paris and all points west. Things quieten down, however, once roads split and the péage is reached.

Here traffic thins out as the thrifty French drivers head for the *routes nationales* which are toll-free.

Two hours or so after leaving the ship I reach the exit which takes me to Bapaume and the road to Albert along which the events of July to November, 1916, unfolded. Passing dark green Commonwealth War Graves Commission (CWGC) signs to cemeteries bearing familiar names, I make my way to Amiens, a city of huge significance during the Great War, and nowadays my base while on the Somme. It is here that my expedition truly begins.

CHAPTER 2

AMIENS

TODAY Amiens is the capital of the Somme Department, part of the ancient region of Picardy. As the largest town in the area with a population approaching 140,000 it has much to offer tourists of all types, not just battlefield visitors. However it's the Great War connection that draws me back year after year.

During the War Amiens was of great importance to the British Army not only as a centre for supplies due to its excellent rail links but also as a safe billet where the troops, especially officers, could draw breath away from the danger zone. After being briefly but brutally occupied by the Germans in 1914, the city remained relatively unscathed until the German Spring Offensive in 1918 when it was saved at the last minute by the dogged resistance of the Australians at nearby Villers-Bretonneux.

Though much has changed since then, the troops might still recognise at least some of the town. Up near the station the Carlton-Belfort Hotel, scene of many a convivial meal for seemingly most of the Great War literati, is still in business and not far away is the undisputed gem of Amiens, the glorious Cathedral. Beautifully maintained, it looks much

better than anyone has the right to expect after nearly 900 years of continual use and occasional bombardment. Before I go in I always have a quiet stroll on the esplanade in front of the great main entrance trying to imagine the sounds, sights and even smells of days gone by, from the pleas of medieval mendicants to the more martial clatter of hobnailed boots, the scent of freshly-lit Woodbines and the laughter of men free for a blessed while to enjoy the basic pleasures of everyday life.

The cool splendour of the interior never fails to impress me as I wander about amidst the parties of tourists, schoolchildren and still, even in these secular times, pilgrims. A creature of habit, I would feel my visit to be incomplete if I didn't pause under the Weeping Angel, perched above the visitors with his head resting on his hand and looking like he's got a most unholy hangover. A medieval mason's little jest perhaps?

Further along, the alleged skull of John the Baptist raises a smile as I'm sure it did for Salome when she danced. Then there's the labyrinth, an intricate maze on the central floor of the cathedral, designed as a training ground for would-be entrants to Heaven. Take my tip, start from Heaven (the centre) and work your way back to the beginning and then amaze and impress friends when next you visit by doing it first time the right way round! Having enjoyed these diversions I push on to the main reason for my visit, the wall plaques connected with the War.

The most personal of these memorials is undoubtedly the one dedicated to the memory of Raymond Asquith. Raymond somehow symbolises just how much was swept away in Britain by the Great War. Born into privilege and with a glittering career in law and society prior to 1914, he met his end near Ginchy on the Somme in September, 1916.

I must admit to having a very ambivalent view towards Asquith and his fellow members of the crème de la crème of Edwardian England who were "in charge" in 1914. I also know that much of what I'm about to write will appear mean-spirited, though if you bear with me you'll perhaps find that I am cognisant of and very sympathetic to the sacrifices made by all classes of society. It's just when I read the appreciation of Raymond's life by John Buchan, a novelist incidentally whom I greatly admire, that I find, shall we say, a little difficulty. First though, let's have a look at who Raymond was and then consider what Buchan wrote in *These For*

Remembrance in 1919 when memory and grief were all too fresh.

Raymond Asquith, the eldest son of Herbert Asquith the future Liberal Prime Minister, was born in 1878. He was educated at Winchester School and Balliol College, Oxford, where he won all the prizes worth winning. According to Buchan he was the epitome of all that was praiseworthy in the Edwardian young gentleman. A true Corinthian, he was successful at everything to which he turned his hand while at the same time giving the impression of not trying. The quintessential amateur, he conformed to the code of his class, studiously avoiding being tagged with the dreaded stigma of "pothunter". In Raymond's day practising to succeed was frowned upon as ungentlemanly though I suspect that quite a few of the sporting nobs would sneak in a bit of training when no one else was looking. It was precisely this attitude which condemned British sportsmen, with a few notable exceptions, to years in the wilderness once the rest of the world had picked up on the games we'd invented. As Buchan puts it:

"Raymond, who won every possible prize, must have worked hard some time or other, but no one could say when... an air of infinite leisure hung about him..."

Unfortunately when it came to relationships Raymond's interpersonal skills, a term which I suspect he would have loathed, seem from today's perspective to have left something to be desired. Buchan once more:

"I do not think he could ever be called popular... In the ordinary he inspired awe rather than liking... his courtesy had no warmth in it... he was apt to be intolerant of mediocrity... There was always a touch of scorn in him for obvious emotion... and all the accumulated lumber of prosaic humanity."

Not your obvious companion, then, for a night down the pub or at the music hall. One wonders how he could possibly have understood the needs of those whom he was to lead once the final game kicked off. In fact, Raymond seems to have had a complete contempt for everybody outside his immediate coterie of friends. He even seems to have extended this attitude to eminent solicitors and "heavy-witted" judges once he took up the law. But now comes the paradox.

Remember that Raymond came from the Asquiths, one of the great Liberal families; the Liberals whose credo was to help the working classes to better themselves. It would appear that at least some of the Party's compassion had rubbed off on him as, when he began to make noises about a political career, Raymond found admirers in none other than J.H. Thomas and other prominent members of the nascent Labour Party. It may well be that his apparent concern for the less fortunate members of society was paternalistic, patronising even, but at least it did exist. Who knows how radicalised he may have become had he been spared the untimely death he met as a subaltern on the Somme? As he revealed in a letter to J.H. Thomas he "sought no privileges not accorded to the ordinary soldier" and felt he belonged among "the close comradeship of his battalion". And it was with those close comrades in the Grenadier Guards that he died on the road from Ginchy to Lesbouefs on September 15, 1916.

Raymond was memorialised thus by Buchan, "Debonair and brilliant and brave, he is now part of that immortal England which knows not age or weariness or defeat".

Perhaps it's best that I leave these last words by Buchan on Raymond to stand uncommented upon. After all

Buchan knew him and his society whereas I do not. I'm also acutely conscious of the fact that any opinions I express are the product of later developments and discoveries, socially, politically and historically, and that I'm being influenced by my own knowledge and beliefs in coming to conclusions that are, perhaps, unfair. The next time I stand before that plaque in Amiens I don't know how I shall feel.

Guilty perhaps that I have by my writing demeaned the memory of a great man and others of his class who died. On the other hand it may well be that I'm only being true to myself and the memory of the thousands of men and women from all across the social spectrum who perished on the battlefields or at base hospitals, sheep betrayed by the very shepherds who should have done more to protect them from the wolves of war. Note that I wrote "betrayed", not "abandoned", as Raymond and his fellow glitterati ended up just as dead as those who became, regardless of class, their comrades in death as they never could have been in life.

Probably because of what I have just written, I shall pay another visit to Raymond's grave in Guillemont Road Cemetery and make amends if any are necessary.

Having now broken the thread of my tour of the Cathedral in no uncertain manner, this is probably as good a time as any to address the question of my cemetery visits though I shall return to the subject in Chapter 13. Why do I go out of my way to stand before a white headstone in a

graveyard far from home?

You know, I don't really have an answer. The best I can come up with is to let the man, or woman, who lies before me 'know' that I remember them and respect them for having done something that I can't even imagine. I touch the stone and talk softly, just saying "I'm here because you're there. I've had all the dawns and sunsets you've missed. So thanks". Pure superstition, of course, and probably completely meaningless. But it isn't to me. I'm not in the least religious nor a believer in the hereafter but there, in the beautifully maintained cemeteries of Flanders and France, I experience spirituality and, especially, peace. In addition, all those dead who are forever young make me realise what an incredibly lucky little chap I've been, never to have faced the prospect of joining them in a very early bath. Like Raymond did.

I finish my cathedral tour by looking at the seven other plaques erected after the War, each one honouring the sacrifices made by the countries of the British Empire and also by the USA. Then it's time to return to the sunlight and set off down to the River Somme and a literary connection.

I suppose that for my generation, the one whose fathers participated in the War, the very word "Somme" evokes a shudder of horror. Ironically, the river herself is a serene old girl flowing gently through the town just as she has done over the centuries.

Nowadays she hosts dinner cruises and picnic outings and holds out the prospect of a catch for the ever hopeful fishermen on her banks, but wind back to those wartime years and she was alive with hospital barges transporting the wounded to the big hospitals at Abbeville and on the coast.

On the far bank of the Somme from the Cathedral runs
the Boulevarde du Cange where lies the house immortalised
by Sebastian Faulks in his novel, *Birdsong*, the first part of
which is concerned with the passionate affair between
Isabelle, a married Frenchwoman and Stephen, a young
Englishman. Isabelle's house isn't hard to find. It's the rather
spooky one behind iron railings with windows peering out
from the thick ivy in which it's covered. The owner is a very
amiable gentleman, at least he was when I was sticking my
camera lens through his front gate. Though he happily
admitted that his dwelling was the model for Faulks' house of
passion, *la maison de rumpy-pumpy*, he was at pains to point
out that there was no red room inside. You'll have to read the
novel to get the significance of that particular fact, I'm afraid.

Now it's time to sit in one of the riverside cafes and sip
a glass of beer reflecting on what's gone and anticipating
what's to come.

Welcome to the House of Fun!

CHAPTER 3

JERICHO AND ALBERT

A beautiful morning and it's off down the Boulevarde d'Alsace Lorraine, over the Somme and up the D929 road which leads to Albert, the gateway to the battlefields. But first there's time for a visit *en route* to a prison and a cemetery. The prison in question is the Amiens Jail which lies on the left hand side of the Albert Road. With its high walls and generally forbidding appearance, it's very easy to spot. Dodging the speeding traffic, I cross over to visit the site of one of the most remarkable rescue missions of World War II, the Amiens Prison Raid, codenamed Operation Jericho. Yes, World War II. I know that I'm meant to be concentrating on the previous conflict but this is an opportunity to pay my respects to some very brave men.

On February 18, 1944, a flight of 18 Mosquito fighter-bombers took off from a snowbound airfield in southern England in an attempt to bring down the walls of Amiens Jail with bombs, hopefully with a result similar to Joshua's stunt with his trumpets at Jericho in Biblical times. The reason for the 1944 attack was that, among the 700 or so inmates languishing behind bars, were 180 Resistance men whose presence was urgently needed to cause diversionary mischief in the build up to the forthcoming D-Day landings. The raid was also designed as a morale booster for the local Resistance who'd had a disastrous winter with betrayal rampant, especially in the Abbeville cell.

An audacious plan was conceived to use the high speed Mosquitoes in a low level attack designed to blow holes in both the outer and inner walls of the prison in the hope that the Resistance men would be able to escape in the ensuing mayhem. The fact that twelve executions had been scheduled for the next day, February 19, to be followed shortly after by others, lent an air of urgency to the planning. Their impending doom by firing squad also ensured that, in case of injury or death caused by the raiders, there would be no complaints from the prisoners since they were condemned to die anyway. Either way the proceedings were going to be incredibly risky for inmates and fliers alike.

Amiens Jail today, showing the repaired main gate and wall.

Under the command of Group Captain "Pick" Pickard, D.S.O., D.F.C., the three squadrons of Mosquitoes left RAF Hunsdon at 1100 hours on the 18th which meant that the attack on the prison would occur at about midday when the prison staff would be at their dinner. Crossing the Channel just above the wave tops in a severe snowstorm, the attackers made landfall near Dieppe and pressed on to Amiens. By this time the weather had greatly improved and so the fliers were able to come in at treetop height as planned, parallel with that road to Albert where today the only hazard is the traffic. After initial misses, the main objectives were achieved. According to plan the guards' canteen took a direct hit and breaches were made in the walls through which prisoners were seen to be escaping. By this time the Germans were on full alert and struck back with anti-aircraft fire and Focke-Wulf 109s from the nearby airfield at Glisy. Of the Mosquitoes involved only two failed to return, one of which was Pickard's. Going back to ride shotgun on the other non-returnee, Pickard was caught by a combination of flak and 109s, giving his life in a vain attempt to help one of his colleagues.

At the time the results of the raid were controversial locally due to widespread collateral damage and the fact that, although 50 Resistance men escaped, so did 179 criminals, while a further 150 prisoners and guards lay dead or wounded. Nevertheless it was, to say the least, a most remarkable feat of arms which, like the Dambusters the year before, meant a great deal in terms of boosting morale both at home and amongst the Resistance. Traces of the attack still remain in the form of the repaired wall to the left of the prison entrance and a shrine and plaque which is dedicated "To the French patriots killed on 18 February, 1944, in this prison, martyred by the barbarous Nazis". And, of course, there are the graves. There are always the graves.

About 200 metres up the road is the St Pierre Cemetery, one of Amiens' municipal graveyards, with a CWGC extension at the back. Here lie Allied bodies mostly from the Great War but also some from World War II, including those of the fliers from the Jericho Raid. The sun was shining through the trees as I walked up the path, the only other people about being three old ladies meticulously cleaning their family vaults. I found "Pick" Pickard's grave quite easily with that of his observer, John Broadley, beside him, together in death as they had been in the cockpit. Pickard was 28 and Broadley 24.

On Pickard's grave is the well-worn epitaph "At the going down of the sun we shall always remember him".

I hope we do.

Back to the car and off up the road to Albert, a town of immense significance to the British during the Great War. It was the nearest Allied railhead to the front line on the Somme and vital for the gathering and distribution of supplies. Today it's still of importance to the British but now as a base for tourists exploring the battlefields of the past.

Albert's Basilica (great church) dominates not only the town but much of the surrounding countryside as well. On a sunny day the Madonna and Infant Christ atop the gilded dome can be seen from almost anywhere on the old battlefields, flashing and sparkling, drawing the eye back to the town and the mind to the wartime legend of the Leaning Virgin. This particular piece of hokum said that if ever the Holy Mother should fall, the War would end shortly thereafter. At that point early in the conflict she was hanging on by the skin of her heavenly teeth as she'd been damaged by shellfire. Wired to the dome by the Royal Engineers she eventually gave up the ghost in April, 1918, after the Germans had taken the town in their Spring Offensive. Mother and child were brought

crashing down by the gunners of the Royal Artillery to discourage the German observers who had established themselves in the tower and with their fall died the legend. The War didn't end. It would take another seven months of bitter fighting before the guns eventually fell silent.

Before heading out of town on the D929 road to Bapaume it's worth taking time to stroll around Albert if only to indulge in one, or more, of the gateaux from the patisserie.

The D929 road is integral to an understanding of the Battle of the Somme as it was in the general direction of this arrow-straight Roman highway that the British and their French allies were meant to proceed on Day One, capturing objectives on the way and ending up, eventually, in Bapaume. Of course, things didn't quite work out like that.

At this juncture I suppose I should provide details of the Battle of the Somme – causes, course, consequences – but I shall refrain from doing so as I'm sure that anyone interested enough to be reading this will have at least a passing knowledge of the subject and its traumatic legacy. So, having spared you a lengthy rehash of the known facts, let's proceed in a north-easterly direction along the road from Albert to the CWGC cemetery at Ovillers and the mystery of John Lauder.

CHAPTER 4

THE MYSTERIOUS DEATH OF CAPTAIN JOHN LAUDER

THE body of Captain John Currie Lauder, beloved son of Sir Harry Lauder, may lie at peace in Ovillers but the controversy which has attached itself to his death refuses to lie down. First, however, before we become embroiled in the myths, speculations and maybe even some facts about John's death, let's have a look at who he was. To do this we have to begin with his father.

For those readers too young to have any knowledge of Harry Lauder, it might come as a surprise to find out that he was, without any doubt, the first international superstar of popular entertainment wherever English was spoken. He was also acknowledged at home as not only Scotland's best-loved entertainer but also its most despised. This paradox, as we shall see, would have a significant effect on how his son's death on the Western Front has since been regarded on his native heath.

Harry was born in Portobello, just outside Scotland's capital, Edinburgh, in 1870, into relatively comfortable circumstances, a situation which was to change with the death of his father. After a spell in Arbroath on Scotland's east coast where he worked in a flax mill and attended school part-time, Harry moved in 1884 to Hamilton, near Glasgow, to work in the coal mines. During this early period of his life, though, he was also keeping his eye firmly upon his real goal – success as an entertainer - by performing in variety theatres all over Central Scotland. Experiments as a light comedian and singer in the English style having proved unsuccessful, Harry

changed tack radically and set out to exploit his Scottishness. Out went the conventional garb of the young man-about-town and in came the tam o' shanter, kilt, sporran, pipe and fantastically crooked walking stick. He became, in fact, the nightmare of every would-be Scottish sophisticate, if such a beast exists. He also became very rich and famous not only in his native land but also abroad.

By dint of good fortune and a great deal of hard work, Harry found himself in exactly the right place at precisely the right time. His heyday was during the first three decades of the twentieth century, a time when technology and circumstance combined to offer him a worldwide stage on which to strut his stuff. The technology was the pioneering advances being made in recorded sound via phonograph rolls and then shellac records. The circumstance was the Scottish diaspora which had begun in the nineteenth century and was still proceeding apace.

Thousands of Scots had over the decades stiffened the backbone of the British Empire both militarily and in the workplace. While Scottish bayonets kept unruly natives in far flung outposts conveniently in their place, Scottish muscle laboured in the factories of the USA, broke the prairies of Canada and brought the farmlands of Australia and New Zealand into production. So there was a ready-made worldwide audience for all things Scottish. However these ex-pats didn't want to be told why they had left behind their often miserable lives in their homeland. No! They were only too eager to devour what Harry Lauder and his successors right up to the present day were only too willing to give them – an idealised vision of a Scotland steeped in the tartan and the cosy croft and positively knee-deep in heather. All this went down a bundle 'abroad', including even England. It also stirred the first signs back home of that tartan kitsch resentment still ongoing today. However, for his fans, and there were millions of them, Harry could do no wrong.

Through his stage persona of the pawky, wee, eternally resilient Scotsman of precarious means, Harry Lauder became fabulously wealthy and gratifyingly famous. Beginning with a hugely successful London debut in 1900 when he unleashed 'I Love a Lassie' on to his adoring English audience, he went on to tour the USA and Canada twenty-two times over the years along with frequent visits to the Antipodes and anywhere else that Scots had settled. What made Harry a superstar was the fact that his appeal spread far beyond Scotland and Scots people into the rest of the English-speaking world which he had reached through the phonograph. His tunes were catchy and his lyrics, though sung in a pronounced Scottish accent, were understandable and appealed to an audience already well versed in Victorian sentimentality. He was one of the pioneers of the recording medium and was the first British entertainer to sell one million units in total sales. Exploiting his success on disc, Lauder toured endlessly both at home and abroad, offering performances that were never less than highly satisfying to his millions of fans. Many years ago I had personal experience of Lauder's enduring international appeal and, if I may indulge my nostalgia, I shall share this with you.

In July, 1963, I rolled, courtesy of Greyhound Buses, into Nashville, Tennessee, on a tour of the USA that might be described at best as that of an innocent abroad. About ten at night I checked into the YMCA where the desk clerk, noting my accent and address, hauled his work-sharing colleague downstairs to meet me. Said colleague was a gentleman of 63 years who, believe it or not, hailed from Clackmannanshire, my home county in Scotland. He'd emigrated to Nashville just after the Great War and was only too eager to talk of Scotland and "the good old days". What emerged from our chat was that the greatest thing he'd seen during his "exile" in Nashville was Harry Lauder's visit in the

1920s to the Athens of the South when he was accorded the kind of downtown parade reserved usually for returning home-grown American heroes. At the time I must admit that this all came as a bit of a shock, to put it mildly, but gradually over the ensuing decades it has begun to make sense. Where better for Harry Lauder to be feted than Nashville, the home of country music, a genre which owes much of its appeal to its roots in the melodies, rhythms and sentiments of the music of Scotland and Ireland? My slightly derisory attitude to Lauder, by the way, was typical of most young Scots of that time and, as we grew older, it became, unfortunately, enshrined in the Scottish psyche. In essence, Harry Lauder and his legacy were bad for Scotland at home and abroad and his image had to be erased from the blackboard of Scottish culture. This attitude is still very prevalent today, making it easy for those with an axe to grind about supposed Scottish dignity to do so against the offending bony knees of Harry Lauder.

If you're beginning to get my rather obvious drift, a head of steam which continues to hiss away today was beginning to build amongst many Scots who were either ashamed of Harry Lauder or, more importantly, jealous of his success. Scots in general have difficulty in acknowledging that one of their own can dare to become successful and popular, especially away from their home turf. This attitude, defined by the Australians as the "Tall Poppy Syndrome", still exists else the tabloids would sell very few copies. People, not just the Scots, love to build up their idols, regarding them almost as personal creations, and then to tear them down at the first sign that they might be "getting above themselves". This particular Rubicon was crossed by Harry when, in 1907, in search of some peace he bought a large mansion in Dunoon, then an upmarket holiday resort on the Clyde coast.

LAUDERVALE, (MR HARRY LAUDER'S RESIDENCE) DUNOON.

He called it "Laudervale" and built a wall round it for privacy, perhaps the first signs for those who chose to see them, that his "man of the people" facade was beginning to crack. Moving with Harry to his Argyllshire Shangri La were, naturally, his wife, Nance, whom he'd married in 1890, and their only son, John, in whom Harry, like many a proud father before and since, had invested all his dreams and pride. And it was through that beloved son and the supposed "mystery" of his death that some Scots would be able to get their revenge, then and now, against the father.

Understandably, Harry doted upon John, ensuring for him the best education that money could buy, first at the City of London School and then Cambridge University. Just to make sure that John's future was completely assured, Harry bought the local Argyllshire estate of Glenbranter for him. Unfortunately for John, his impending lairdship might have had quite a bearing on his eventual fate in France, the suggestion being that some of his future tenants in the ranks of his company could have been harbouring a deep resentment against their prospective landlord. It should be noted, however, that the final purchase of Glenbranter with surrounding properties including an island in Loch Eck was not finalised until November, 1916, barely a month before John's death. Whatever, these plans for John's future would assume less significance with the outbreak of war in August, 1914.

John, an accomplished pianist who sometimes accompanied his father, was actually in Australia on tour with him when war broke out. Immediately upon hearing the news, John, as a dutiful reserve officer, set sail for home to prepare to contribute to the war effort. What was this young man like and how had he become part of the peacetime army?

With Laudervale in Dunoon as his home base, Harry made sure that he established himself as a pillar of the local community, the high wall notwithstanding. John also became involved in the social whirl and enlisted, as would be expected of him, as a subaltern in the 8th Battalion of the Argyll and Sutherland Highlanders (A&SH), the local Territorials, in 1912. As a Territorial John retained his civilian status but was expected to attend training sessions and, especially, the annual summer camp. He seems to have thrown himself into his new role with great enthusiasm if the following postcard depicting him, kilt flying, leading his grinning men in a mock charge, is anything to go by.

The men whom young Lauder commanded were from the immediate locality around Dunoon, bound together by strong bonds of kinship, friendship or common experience. John, unfortunately, could lay claim to no such ties being an incomer, separated further from his men by his father's wealth and reputation and by his own education. Nevertheless John's military career seems to have progressed satisfactorily from

Harry Lauder's Son Leads a charge of Argyll Highlanders.

part-time training prior to 1914 to full-time soldiering with the outbreak of war. Indeed, by 1916, he had been promoted to Captain.

In the summer of that year of the Somme John had become engaged to Mildred Thomson, a joyous event for the Lauders, and it was this union which had prompted Harry to buy the aforementioned 20,000 acre Glenbranter Estate for the presumably happy couple.

Unfortunately, neither the marriage nor the lairdship was to be consummated. Captain John Lauder was killed, aged 25, on 28 December, 1916, near Courcelette on the Somme. And thereby hangs the supposed mystery. Did he fall in the course of doing his duty at the front or was he pushed by one of his own men? Was it a bullet from the rifle of a German sniper, a mine explosion or a shot in the back from a disgruntled Jock which cut short his life?

Though I'd been aware of Harry Lauder all my life, the fate of his son was completely unknown to me until 1996 when *Empty Footsteps*, a novel by Lorn McIntyre, was reviewed in the Scottish press. And it is to this book and author that most of the current controversy, if controversy there be, can be attributed. In fact, so far as the present is concerned, all roads lead to Lorn. This being the case, it might behove us to have a look at what he says. First though, a word of caution. I fully understand that *Empty Footsteps* is a novel, a work of fiction, and should be judged on its merits as such, a job which is outwith my compass. However, when an author uses a real person as a character then he/she must take some responsibility for the impression made by this character on the reader. This is especially true in the case of John Lauder in *Empty Footsteps* where McIntyre's creation and his suggested fate is a major thread of the book.

We first meet John Lauder at the annual battalion sports day in Dunoon prior to the outbreak of war where he is revealed to be a junior officer keen to throw his somewhat light weight about in an attempt to appear manly before his fiancée and assembled guests. Described as "the slightly built lieutenant with dubious eyesight", he appears frail, especially when contrasted with one of his men, Mr Life-force himself, Dochie McDougall, a worker from the Glenbranter Estate. Lauder is depicted from the outset as unable to relate to his men not only because of his personality and upbringing but

also by the fact that most of the soldiers are bilingual and not above using the Gaelic to exclude those, like their lieutenant, whom they see as "outsiders". Somewhat sadly John states, "I joined the Territorials to make friends…" – something, if the author is to be believed, he completely failed to do.

The growing conflict between John and his men is exacerbated by the purchase of Glenbranter as John's plans for the future of the estate hinge on his intention "to buy a lot of sheep", something that would enrage his men, especially those who are his tenants. Here McIntyre plugs into one of the great perceived injustices of Scottish history, the Highland Clearances of the 19th century, when the "great sheep" replaced people over vast swathes of the Highlands. So from the beginning we have John on the other side of the cultural fence from the men he would be leading into battle. He is also depicted as being rather inept with women unlike the aforementioned Dochie who relates in a very positive way to anything presentable in a skirt. Indeed the whole scenario centres on this division between the almost effete Lauder and the robust common soldiery under his command, who often come across, though I'm not sure that this is the author's intention, as little more than bullies. By the time they arrive in the trenches, the relationship between officer and men has not improved and Dochie is presented as an ever growing threat to Lauder, describing him as "a weed".

The author also has an axe to grind about Harry Lauder, portraying him as a jumped up *nouveau riche*, described by one of the more sympathetic of the characters, Hector Macdonald the piper, as "the bugger with the crooked stick". Meanwhile poor old John seems to go from bad to worse as the war and the novel progresses. Even when he's wounded he receives no sympathy, especially, as might be expected, from Dochie who describes his officer as "a lazy bugger" adding that he hopes that "the bastard" is "kept at home for good". By this time it is becoming clear that Dochie is assuming the role of Lauder's nemesis and we all know where that one leads.

To be fair to Lorn McIntyre, his largely unsympathetic portrayal of Captain Lauder is tempered by the suggestion that the young man desperately wants to succeed both as a soldier and as a man, a wish thwarted by circumstances and what we are shown to be his personal shortcomings. However I'm pretty sure that by now you can see the path down which the author has been leading us. John Lauder, disliked by all and despised by some, is about to "get his", one way or another. And the opportunity arises at Courcelette on the Somme in late December, 1916, most probably but never definitely, courtesy of Dochie, who conveniently has his head blown off the following year. Although the author allows the reader to make up his or her own mind as to the cause of Lauder's death, sniper or assassin, the "evidence" definitely leans toward the latter scenario. McIntyre, himself from Argyll, apparently has claimed that it is 'common knowledge' there that John Lauder was shot by one of his own men.

Similar in tone and, I suspect, based largely if not totally on *Empty Footsteps*, is the Scottish website *firstfoot.com*. Choosing to go down the sensational route, the writers set out their stall from the very beginning with the title, "Captain John C. Lauder (Exit Stage Left 1916)". When they go on to describe the stage act of Lauder Senior as "demeaning" and the man himself as "this jumped-up music hall singer who got rich ridiculing his countrymen", it quickly becomes obvious whose side these particular "critics" are on. They declare that Harry used his influence to get John a commission in the Territorials, "a fitting position for a laird's son", without stopping to consider that John, with his education and position in local society, would have been expected to assume the basic officer rank of Second Lieutenant without any backroom work necessary by his father. (We'll deal with the matter of John's wartime promotion later.) Further, John is described as "a haughty disciplinarian... and... disliked intensely by his men..." without a shred of evidence being put forward. His death is implied to be mysterious being the only one on the 28 December, 1916, when there were no enemy attacks. No consideration is given to the fact that snipers were a constant threat throughout the War, especially during such quiet periods as existed in late December 1916 near Courcelette. These men, the snipers, were the pros of the Western Front, capable and skilled, and always on the lookout for their next score. Why should one on December 28 not have been at the expense of John Lauder? The website entry finishes with the insinuation that he was killed by his own men but employs the get-out clause, "Although there are no official records, the story is strongly entrenched and part of local folklore in Argyll..." This is followed by the question, "Is it true? Did J.C. Lauder get what was coming to him?" The compilers then refer to *Empty Footsteps*, stating that "the story has also since appeared there" – implying, I think, that this gives it some sort of authenticity. These two sources may well have some elements of truth contained within them but I feel that before their "revelations" sully the Lauder name further, some delving in the mud of memory and actual evidence might be in order. And where better to begin than in Dunoon itself, the town John came to regard as home.

Dunoon Castle Museum

On a sparkling autumn day I visited this onetime
"Jewel of the Clyde" where Captain Lauder's name is just one
of many on the town war memorial. The lady at the local
tourist office was very pleasant, revealing that her
grandmother had been a very close friend of John's mother,
Nance. She knew a great deal about the Lauders in Dunoon
but nothing, apart from the official version, "Killed In
Action", of the manner of John's death. Extending my search,
I went to the Castle Museum, which, by the way, is well
worth a visit if only for, and there's a little touch of irony
here, its exhibit on Harry Lauder. There I met with three
locals, habitués of the museum. Pleasant, friendly chaps in
their fifties, they stated quite categorically that John Lauder
had indeed been shot by one of his own men. No messing.
Definite. "Common knowledge [that phrase again] in the
area", they said. Their evidence? Shortly before they died
some of the local survivors of the 8th Argylls had "opened

up" to their families after years of a conspiracy of silence on the subject. The fact that Lorn McIntyre had been in Dunoon just a few days prior to my visit lecturing on the Lauders and the possibilities of John's death simply added grist to their rumour mill. They seemed, genuinely, to be totally convinced. But on what grounds? Hearsay and whispers inspired by any number of motives, some of which we touched on earlier – but no actual names.

And now we come to the crux. There is, as might be expected in the absence of a court martial, no documentary evidence to substantiate any of the allegations of murder. There is, however, quite a bit of well-documented speculation about Lauder's death, investigation of which might prove more fruitful than local legend and a work of fiction – or should that be "faction"?

What, if anything, is known for sure? The only solid facts that I've been able to dig up are contained in the mud-stained pages of the Regimental Diary held in the Argyll & Sutherland Highlanders Museum at Stirling Castle. These reveal that December, 1916, had been a relatively quiet time in the Courcelette sector and the 28th of the month conformed to that pattern. The terse "Summary of Events and Information" states, "A&D Companies in trenches. Captain J.C. Lauder killed. One O.R. wounded".

Because there is no further "official" evidence, just this simple report of an everyday occurrence on the Western Front, the conspiracy of silence theorists and assorted others have had their field days ever since. The first of these in print, at least so far as I can detect, was the ever gregarious Jack House, "Mr Glasgow" himself.

Twenty years before the publication of *Empty Footsteps*, the subject of Captain Lauder's death arose in the

Diary column of the *Glasgow Herald* in connection with House's biographical play about Harry Lauder which premiered at the Citizens Theatre, Glasgow, on May 11, 1976. This time the cause of John Lauder's untimely end was alleged to be due to nothing more than his own overweening arrogance. While researching his play, House claimed to have been visited, separately, by two "independent" witnesses to the shooting of John Lauder whose stories matched. The gist of their accounts was that John Lauder insisted that, when an enemy trench was taken, all its occupants were to be shot and this was what had happened just prior to his death. He had led a successful assault, presumably had all survivors shot and, delighted with his success, was dancing a Highland Fling on the parapet when he was downed by a German sniper. Well, at least it was a Hun who had done the deed, not one of his own men. But young Lauder still comes out of it, or, rather, didn't come out of it, looking a proper Charlie.

Objection Number One – Why would any officer order the total annihilation of prisoners when everybody knew that they were in great demand as sources of intelligence with consequent kudos to said officer? Also such a policy would bring with it inevitable reciprocal retaliation by the enemy. Undoubtedly prisoners on all sides were shot out of hand but this was in the heat of combat. You only have to study the many photos taken at the time of German prisoners being used as stretcher bearers and in other non-combatant roles on their way back to the British rear areas to realise that the shooting of captives was not a general policy. Was Lauder so much out of touch with reality that he was waging his own personal war with his own rules? Highly unlikely.

Objection Number Two – John Lauder may or may not have been an unpopular officer but he was definitely an experienced one and dancing about on battlefields would not be part of his repertoire. Playing the piano in the rest areas maybe, but jigging at the front...? So what are we to make of this "evidence"? I'm quite happy with the German sniper bit but common sense dictates that the leaping about is a bit far-fetched. Good publicity for the play, though, and wasn't it Jack the Lad himself who stated that he had never let a concern for the facts get in his way if there was a good story to be told?

Nevertheless, some good did come from setting this particular hare running. At least the culprit had been identified as a German sniper, not one of the 8th Argylls. There followed some lively correspondence in the *Herald* which revealed how witnesses can interpret "facts" in totally different ways, especially when they're viewed through the twin fogs of war and failing memory.

James McWhirter, 83 years old in 1976, was in the 6th Battalion A&SH in the same sector as Lauder. He contended, probably accurately, that "shot by your own men" is a soldiers' myth revived in every war. Such acts might occur but surely only when bullets are flying around ensuring that the perpetrator would not be identified. He also dismissed as fantasy the idea of Lauder's war dance. Unfortunately his own information that Lauder was killed with several of his men by the detonation of a German mine just does not stack up against the bare facts stated in the regimental diary – Captain Lauder killed, one O.R. wounded. No other casualties in the section on that day.

Through the rest of May, 1976, information on the subject kept cropping up in the paper. In that very first article there is a reference to Harry Lauder's distress that a rumour had begun that John might have been shot by one of his own men. It's interesting to note that the first veteran to come on board, Mr McWhirter, dismissed such a theory out of hand and even more interesting to discover that no further 'evidence' to this effect would appear in the ensuing correspondence. Further suggestions as to the cause of John's death were, however, proffered.

Charles Black, a private in Lauder's "A" Company on the fateful day, stated quite definitely in the *Herald* of May 21, 1976, that John Lauder was sniped by the enemy. According to Charles and other sources there had been a post-Christmas lull in the fighting in the Courcelette-Pozières sector at the time, probably due to the bitterly cold weather. Apart from the occasional shell being fired just to remind the troops on both sides that there was a war going on, little was happening. It was Lauder's bad luck that one of these rounds landed nearby and failed to explode. Realising that it was a dud, he went out to bring it in. Just at that point, nearby British troops decided to lob a rifle grenade at the Germans in retaliation for this breach of the peace, an action which, in turn, attracted the attention of the Huns' resident sniper. As Lauder was the only available target, he was duly put away. This, by the way, is the version that Sir Harry would eventually accept as the truth.

"Ah," I hear you ask, "what kind of idiot goes out to bring in a dud shell?" However it would appear that Captain Lauder was merely doing his duty in retrieving the shell. Orders were in place that any such misfires should be retrieved in order that the timing fuse in the nose cap could be studied by British Intelligence. They could then calculate the position of the gun which had fired the device and bring down retribution upon it. So, far from being an idiot, Captain Lauder was doing his duty, choosing to take the risk upon himself rather than expose one of his men to danger. This account was confirmed in the same issue of the *Herald* by Alistair Meighan, whose father was the medical officer who tried to save John Lauder's life.

John Macleod of Skye, a Seaforth Highlander in a nearby position, claimed in a later letter to the Herald in 1986 that he had actually seen an officer of the A&SH in the open wearing his officer's light-coloured trench coat, providing a target which would be irresistible to a German sniper. Normally officers would not be so foolish as to wear such a garment at the front but John Lauder apparently was set to go on leave and so might well have had it with him to wear on the journey home. With the cold as intense as reported, it's also possible that he made the unfortunately fatal decision to wear it over his outer clothing. Why the subject of Lauder's death had been returned to ten years after the first flurry of correspondence, I was not able to confirm. Perhaps it was the last testament of a very old man who wanted to tell the truth as he had seen it. Whatever the reason, John Macleod was convinced that a German sniper had shot John Lauder.

For me, the most convincing account of John's death comes from a very significant eye witness, his batman, George Tait, a Dunoon man, who would, presumably, be aware of the resentment among local men about the Captain, if indeed it existed. Tait confirms the unexploded shell/German sniper story though he states that Lauder had merely left the trench "to have a look", not to retrieve the shell. According to William Wallace in his book *Harry Lauder in the Limelight*, Tait's version of the incident never varied. "This is the story always given by George Tait who returned to Dunoon and he maintained it to his dying day". That Tait was very aware of the alternative version is obvious from the following:

"...There were others who circulated the false rumour that Captain Lauder was unpopular with his men and one of them had shot him. This nasty and malicious tale grieved Harry Lauder very much and upset many of John Lauder's friends, most of all batman Tait."

So what are we left with? The strongest of probabilities is that Captain Lauder was shot by a German sniper while doing his duty. The only "mystery" that presents itself is the possibility that he was unpopular due to his snooty and bullying manner. So let's see what kind of character references we're left with after we extract the contributions of Lorn Macintyre and those supposedly "in the know" in Dunoon today.

First of all, John loved being in Dunoon, "enjoying", according to Wallace, "the contrast from the Cambridge campus", which suggests that John felt at home in the area. Surely if he was disliked by all and sundry he would have ensured that any visits he made to Argyllshire would have been infrequent and short. And he certainly would have been unlikely to have joined the local Territorials when he could have realised any martial ambitions he might have had in the Cambridge University O.T.C. The postcard showing him leading his apparently merry men does not portray a deeply disliked junior officer. John also seems to have been accepted by his fellow officers at the front, accompanying their singsongs on piano during breaks in the fighting.

Second, the available evidence suggests that John Lauder was, at the very least, an efficient officer who had certainly seen action. According to army records, John was promoted to Lieutenant in April, 1914 and to Captain in

October, 1915. Much has been made of the fact that John was promoted due to his father's influence. The facts are as follows. His original rank on joining the Territorials, Second Lieutenant, was the normal entrance rank to the military for one of John's social class. His promotion to Lieutenant in 1914 suggests satisfactory progress in the Territorials while his advancement to Captain confirms that, as a soldier, he was doing the job correctly. If John Lauder had been incompetent or unable to manage his men it is highly unlikely that he would have reached the rank of Captain as a frontline officer. Rather he would have been kept back and given a job where he could do as little damage as possible. This, I have been told by military sources, was a recognised but unofficial procedure. Ironic really that failure could sometimes keep an officer relatively safe. This was not the case for John who, after convalescence in 1916, was sent to bombing school where he became an instructor, not a role bestowed upon dummies I would have thought.

Shortly after John had been promoted to Captain, he had been invalided home suffering from shrapnel wounds, dysentery and shell-shock. Despite being, according to his father, severely debilitated by his experiences, he returned to the front later in 1916, eager, once again according to Harry, to get back to his men. Lest one reads into this home leave some kind of preferential treatment being accorded John on account of his father's influence, this pattern of recovery, if indeed recovery occurred, was common for officers. Their men, unfortunately, were more likely to have to rely on a slightly more serious "Blighty One" to get them back to Britain. Which brings us to the question of Harry's supposed influence.

There seems to be among the anti-Lauder faction a general belief that John's continuing promotion was largely due to his father. In fact this kind of influence cut little ice after Haldane's Army Reforms in 1908. Just look at the struggle Rudyard Kipling had to get his own son, ironically also named John, into the forces at all, never mind a commission. By 1915 the upward path to promotion had been widened by the horrendous toll of frontline officers making any influence, parental or otherwise, largely irrelevant. Quite simply, John wouldn't have needed his father's backing. Unfortunately, as we have seen, John, not long after receiving his captaincy, was to become just another statistic.

Obviously, after all the time that's elapsed, I've no real idea what kind of man or officer John Lauder was but going on what I've been able to discover I'm pretty sure he was not shot by one of his own men nor was he celebrating a massacre of the enemy. I'm sorry to disappoint the conspiracy theorists out there but the available evidence points in a completely different direction, one that leads to the conclusion that John was just another victim of the insatiable war machine, simply killed at the front like thousands of others before and after. And what about that "after"? What happened once John was laid to rest in the cemetery at Ovillers, not far from where he died? John's story didn't just stop with the sniper's bullet, at least not for his father. Or for Mildred.

At the London hotel where he was residing during his hugely successful run at the Shaftesbury Theatre, Harry was told of John's untimely demise on New Year's Day, 1917. His wife being in Scotland, he was joined in his grief by Mildred, who lived with her parents in the capital. At first Harry felt he couldn't go back on stage but, trouper that he was, he honoured the old showbiz adage, "The show must go on", and returned to the boards only three days later. Too much money and too many people depended on him. Predictably, emotions ran riot both with Lauder and his audience, especially when he broke into the hit number from the show, "The Laddies Who Fought and Won" and even more so when he introduced "Keep Right on to the End of the Road" into his act shortly afterwards.

Later in 1917, once the London run was over, he embarked for France on a mission to raise the morale of the men at the front. His work-rate was prodigious. Not only did he complete a gruelling tour, often in danger from shell-fire, but he also found time to write a bestseller about his experiences, *A Minstrel in France*, which was published early in 1918. And, of course, he also found time to visit John's grave at Ovillers.

Ovillers Cemetery

"We set out across a field that had been ripped and torn by shell fire. All about us there were little brown mounds, each with a white wooden cross upon it. All over, the valley was thickly sown with white crosses... And my own grief was altered by the vision of grief that had come to so many others... In the presence of so many evidences of grief and desolation, a private grief sank into its true perspective. It was no less keen, the agony at the thought of my boy was as sharp as ever. But I knew that I was only one father... God help us all!"

No matter what your opinion of Harry Lauder or his son might be, his description of his visit is extremely poignant, especially as he nears the military cemetery where his son lies. Any of you out there who have undertaken grave visits either for or with descendants of the fallen will recognise the feeling of anticipation and dread as the site comes ever nearer. For us, the feeling is one of a task completed and a debt fulfilled, especially if you know that yours is the first visit to have been made to that particular grave. Imagine then what must have been the experience of a "first generation" visitor like Harry Lauder.

"So we came, when we were, perhaps, a mile from the Bapaume Road, to a slight eminence, a tiny hill that rose from the field. A little military cemetery crowned it... Five hundred British boys lie sleeping in that small acre of silence, and among them is my own laddie. There the fondest hopes of my life, the hopes that sustained and cheered me through many years lie buried."

And then the climax, far greater than anything the theatre could offer, the final reality for so many parents, wives, lovers, the end of a quest and yet the beginning of a lifetime of remembering and grieving:

"I went alone to my boy's grave and flung myself down on the warm, friendly earth... I was utterly spent. He was such a good boy!"

And that, my friends, says it all, I think. As Harry remembers John as an infant, anyone who has ever cared about a child can feel for him and be almost glad that he had found there, on a hillside in France, "a sort of tragic consolation". However, just as he was finding this consolation, Lauder was also beginning to be aware of rumblings of the rumour that would torment him for years to come.

In the years immediately following John's death, soldiers who had served with him were to visit Lauder, now Sir Harry in recognition for his efforts in France and also in raising money for disabled Scottish servicemen. And all of them told him the same thing:

> "...That there was not a man in his company who did not feel his death as a personal loss and bereavement. And his superior officers have told me the same thing... All that we have heard of John's life in the trenches and of his death, was such a report as we or any other parents would want to have of their boy."

Sir Harry's assessment of his son's popularity and character reflects, as one might expect, very favourably upon "his boy". However, if only a small part of it is true, it rather contradicts the picture painted in other sources, especially *Empty Footsteps*.

> "John never lost his rare good nature. There were times when things were going very badly... but at such times he could always be counted on to raise a laugh and uplift the spirits of his men."

And perhaps most significant:

> "He knew them all; he knew them well. Nearly all of them came from his home region near the Clyde and so they were his neighbours and his friends."

Hardly, in other words, the kind of men who would want to take a shot at their officer.

One incident, reported in his diary by a "friend and fellow officer", Hugh Munro, describes how John, in July, 1915, when "the spirit of his men was dashed", found a piano in a ruined house at La Gorgue and played and sang some of his father's songs to amazing effect. Munro also reveals how he and other officers, including John, had "a hilarious night" in an old schoolhouse, an event which would no doubt have proved to be a welcome relief from the dangers faced by the nocturnal working parties of which John was a regular member.

Other stories reflecting favourably upon John emerge from the visits paid by his former trenchmates to Sir Harry:

> "Many soldiers and officers of the Argyll and Sutherland Highlanders pass the hoose [sic] at Dunoon... None ever passes, though without dropping in for a bite and sup... to tell us stories of our beloved boy."

OK, so some of those might have just been visiting for a free dram and a bit of shortbread plus the sovereign liberated from the clutches of Sir Harry's sporran on receipt of a favourable report, but the majority must have been genuine. Why? The men of the 8th Argylls mostly came, remember, from the surrounding area, where such visits would be well known and the "liars", if indeed they were such, would be held in contempt.

Sir Harry himself accepted fully the account, substantiated by John's batman, of his son's death – killed by an enemy sniper. But just to make sure and to confound the damnable rumours, he employed private detectives to seek out contrary evidence, if any existed. None was discovered.

So what are we left with? John Lauder shot by one of his own men? Logic and the available evidence emphatically suggest otherwise. John Lauder an unpleasant authoritarian bully? Unlikely, but who knows? Perhaps he was just an ordinary young man thrust, like thousands of others, into extraordinary situations by the Great War, situations for which nothing could prepare them. Who knows how he would react? But remember, John was promoted to Captain and given charge of a company, hardly the mark of an officer unable to handle his men.

Sadness hadn't finished with Harry Lauder with John's death, however. His beloved wife, Nance, who had endured years of sadness after John's demise, died in a post-operative relapse in 1927 delivering to Harry a blow almost equal to that of the loss of his son. From then until he came to the end of his own particular road in 1950, he lived a quiet life at Lauder Ha' in Strathaven, well removed from the sadness and failed hopes of Glenbranter. During these twilight years he became like a godfather to the folk in showbusiness and many famous entertainers, especially Americans, paid him visits, eager to touch the hem of the kilt worn

by one of the greatest of them all.

Mildred never married. Three years after her death in 1975, the Lauder-Thomson Ward was opened at Erskine Hospital which cares for disabled ex-service personnel. It was paid for by Mildred in memory of the man whom she'd loved but never had time to wed.

Mildred, John and Nance Lauder

Throughout her long life, she, like Harry, would "never be far away from the little cemetery hard by the Bapaume Road".

Though John would never have the chance to prove himself as laird of Glenbranter, he's remembered there to this day. On a hillock overlooking his beloved estate is a tiny graveyard in which lies the body of

Nance close by the memorial erected to John by his father.

Ironically, for a man so close to his family in life, Harry is nowhere near to them in death. He's buried in Hamilton, the town where he'd worked in the mines, met and married Nance and first trod the boards as a serious entertainer.

So there you have it – John at peace on a hillside on the Somme, Nance surrounded by nature on a little hill in Argyll and Harry, far removed from the ones he loved so much, in the impersonal vastness of a communal cemetery in a town which has seen better days. Like those when Harry was starting out.

But that's not quite the end. Let me share with you the following very interesting information which was brought to my notice on March 17, 2009, when I was contacted from New York by James Marturano to whom I offer my heartfelt thanks for his generosity. What immediately follows is his e-mail in a slightly edited form. Bob Bain, who is referred to by

James, is the Secretary of the Scottish Music Hall and Variety Theatre Society, formerly the Harry Lauder Society. He is also an extremely interesting and pleasant gentleman with an encyclopaedic knowledge of the Scottish Variety Theatre.

"I was referred to your website by Bob Bain and was much interested to read your chapter on John Lauder. As Bob will tell you, I am a big fan of Sir Harry Lauder and I found your chapter on him to be a very honest and clear-eyed examination of both Sir Harry and his unfortunate son. Neither saints nor sinners – like most of us.

My reason for writing to you is to see if you would be interested in transcriptions of two of John Lauder's letters to his fiancée, Mildred Thomson. One of the letters is, I believe, the last letter he ever wrote, dated 26 December, 1916. The letters were obtained a few years ago from a London man who purchased some of Miss Thomson's furniture in an auction sale. At the time of the auction he had been told that all of Miss Thomson's letters from John Lauder had been destroyed, apparently on the wishes of Miss Thomson and he thought no more of it. Sometime later he took some drawers out of a small nightstand and these four letters fell out from behind. This was in the late 1970s and he kept them these many years. Apparently he took them to the Imperial War Museum where he was told they were authentic but the Museum was otherwise not interested in them. When I returned home and actually read the letters I must confess I began to feel ill at ease. I did not like having them. They seemed too personal and I do not know what to do about them. I feel it is wrong to have them because of Miss Thomson's wishes but also I do not think it right to destroy them because they are part of history."

Naturally I jumped at the chance to have access to such fascinating and moving documents, the only surviving remnants of yet another love story torn asunder by the Great War. I have taken it upon myself to edit the two letters as some phrases, due to the ravages of time, are impossible to decipher. However I can assure you, the reader, that I have not altered in any way their substance.

The first letter, written during John's first tour of duty, reveals something of his existence at the front and also his obvious fondness for Mildred to whom he is not yet engaged. Although some of John's opinions might strike us in these politically correct times as definitely non-PC, it's more than likely that they were pretty typical of many young British subalterns trapped by duty in the muddy fields and shattered villages of Picardie:

Still in the same place in France,
7/5/15

I have never been so jolly delighted to have a letter from anyone as when I got yours yesterday – it was my first (and only) communication from friends at home.

Sorry I had to miss writing to you yesterday but I had time only to write to Father and Mother. I have never been so busy in my life – absolutely fed up with work in every form and guise... If you can find time to write every day I shall be glad, as it is nice to hear from you.

It is rather curious being here, able to hear the guns and knowing that every now and then some men are being sent to perdition – without any ceremony and perhaps incomplete at that!

The country is marshy and absolutely alive with frogs of the croaking type.

Our food is not very excellent. The water here is filthy and must be boiled before use – the natives are a dirty lot (and) wash all sorts of things in their water supply! Our staple diet, as I have told you, is bully beef – at times we get ham, the same as issued to the men, and once we have had fresh meat[?]!

This morning I was up at 3.45 and "stood to arms" until 5.30 am. It is 2.15 pm now and I have been on the move ever since.

Today is not so warm and the rain has kept off.

You can write as long letters and as many as you like – there is no censor to fear!

Our letters are censored, though, as a matter of fact, our word is accepted that there is nothing of military importance therein.

I may find time to continue this letter later but, in case I do not, shall conclude.

With fondest love,

Ever,

John

Well Darling, it is now 5 pm and for once I believe I shall have an hour to myself. But even now I have been working, with hour breaks for breakfast and lunch, for 13 hours!

It has begun to rain again, just a little. It is rather annoying, as one cannot empty one's valise and sort of settle down for a while.

By the bye, this ink I am using is made from ink tablets. It is improving as I write – fortunately.

I have the rather disagreeable job of censoring my Platoon's letters. The O.C. Coy. ought to do it but there are such numbers that we each have to take our own men's.

There is little information any of them can give as they scarcely know what part of the world they are in. One of my NCOs has just asked me if I will accept his word that there is nothing stated in his letters... and would I pass them without reading them.

I am glad to know you are attending church. Your attendance may help to counteract the evils of my life. Living in a stinking village with smelly people and no pyjamas to soothe my army blanket... and having to get up at 4 am and eat bully beef... all tend towards the downward path.

In your letters, just say anything you want to... it will all go to making a nice long chatty epistle.

I am hoping to have another letter from you this evening! Shall I? I have not heard from my people yet.

Glad to know your spring cleaning is over for another season: You will have no excuse for overworking for a while. Tell your father I will write to him one day soon. I shall not be able to answer all his questions!

Shall close for the day.

Fondest love,

Ever

John

The second letter below shows, I think, a deepening of John's feelings for Mildred. They had, after all, become engaged in the early summer of 1916 prior to John's return to active service from his convalescence at home. He obviously was living what I would guess was the typical life of a young officer, better than that of his men but certainly not without a fair share of their discomforts and dangers. What is most significant and poignant about this letter is that it is, so far as we know, the last time John would touch home base. Interestingly it corrects the supposition advanced by John Macleod in 1986 in his correspondence to the *Glasgow Herald* that John was about to go off on leave when he was killed and was therefore wearing his officer's coat ready for a quick getaway to the train. The letter clearly shows that no such leave was imminent.

France
26/12/16

Sweetheart Mine,

I have just had breakfast in bed and am waiting for my shaving water to come. My, if only I had hold of you now, I should squeeze and cuddle you something awful!

Xmas has passed and now New Year is rushing down on us. The days go by very rapidly; nevertheless it is ages since I saw you last, slowly fading from view, waving a white kerchief. I felt jolly sad that night. My shaving water is present and correct so I shall carry on.

Later, Sweetheart, until later in the day.
John, xx

12.50 am

The present 2nd in Command is going on leave today and is then going as instructor at a CO's school at home for several months. I hear that Major Lockie, the permanent 2nd in Command, is not likely to return for a while, so I am wondering whether I am to be taken on as 2nd in command. It seems quite likely as this morning, when the CO was away for a while, he told me to answer for him.

4.40 pm

It seems uncertain whether I shall be 2nd in Command. At present... a still more junior Captain, who has been out all the time, has the job. But I have to go in the trenches in this wet spell (tomorrow) and shall be i/c of the firing there – 2 Coys. in. There are only 2 Captains in the Battalion now and the other one, at present 2nd in command, will likely have to go in with the remaining 2 Coys. when I come out. Then perhaps I shall get the job. It does not matter very much really, but it is rather a disagreeable thing to have a junior officer put over one and being only a kid of 21 or 22.

It is raining again and we do not look forward with much glee to going in tomorrow night as the line is just the same as it was last time.

I am fairly busy getting things ready for the line – there are many things to look after. "Gum boots, thigh, men for the use of" as they are termed, gas respirators and food etc., etc. I believe this is the worst part of life on the 13th front just now, and that means something. However we are all looking forward to the much needed Div. rest, which is more or less promised about January 13th 1917 – NOT 1918!

7.10 pm

This letter consists of spasms today and so may be somewhat disjointed. It is still raining and does not look like improving tonight at least. Dinner is announced so I must away again.

> Love
> John

Must close Darling as it is after midnight – I have been very busy this evening.

> All my very fondest love and kisses.
> Ever thine,
> John

P.S. I may not be able to write to you for 2 or even 4 days but, of course, if possible at all I shall do so.

> All my love
> John

There they stand, testaments of a time long gone. Make of them what you will. My own impression is that they show a young man desperately trying to stay in touch with the reality of everyday life and clinging on to future hopes as a means of preserving his sanity in an otherwise crazy world.

* * *

John Lauder's Box

During the course of my research on John Lauder I had occasion to use the Scottish Theatre Archive at the University of Glasgow. There, among all the paper-based evidence, was one very solid wooden artefact, a box which had been presented by Harry Lauder to John on the occasion of his 11th birthday. Let me describe it to you.

Box Exterior

It's made of brown wood, probably a light mahogany veneer.

Its dimensions are 15 inches (wide) x 10 inches (broad) x 9 inches (deep), approximately.

There are brass protectors on all four corners (top) with bands of brass anchoring the sides near the bottom.

There is a small brass plaque on the top bearing the following inscription:

> John Lauder
> Athole House
> Longley Road
> Tooting
> London

Box Interior

Handwritten in ink on an interior lid, made of plywood, are these words:

> To my son John for his 11th Birthday
> From his Papa
> With Dearest Love

The handwriting is 'educated' – firm, clear, precise.

Under the writing are three drawings of plants coloured in with, I think, wax crayons. Presumably these were added by John.

The interior lid opens up to form a writing desk with a navy blue velvet inlay.

There are three slots for a pen, ink bottle and pen nibs.

The pen is still there with its ink-stained wooden 'shaft' and a cork 'grip' into which the nib is inserted. The nib is badly bent almost as if someone had been trying to play darts with it! The interior opens further to reveal a compartment containing one sheet of writing paper with a watermark of a pseudo-heraldic device and, in German, the word "Gohrsmuhle", presumably the trademark and name of the manufacturer.

It's very hard to express how I felt handling these links with the past. Sad, privileged, excited – and sad once again.

I don't know whether or not John had this box with him at the front though I suppose it's possible since officers carried with them all sorts of extras denied to the other ranks.

The box is in the Harry Lauder Archive which was left to the University by Jimmy Logan, one of the great figures of the Scottish entertainment scene in the latter half of the twentieth century. During the 1980s he toured very successfully with his self-penned show *Lauder*, and it was during its run at a local arts complex that I met him – standing patiently in the queue waiting for his turn to be served at a local fish and chip shop! He was a great chap and is sadly missed.

Lastly, here are two images which bring us closer to John Lauder, courtesy once again of James Marturano of New York.

The first is a view of Dunoon sketched by John from "Laudervale". I don't know when it was done but I'd like to think it was during his last home visit in 1915/16.

The second is an envelope addressed to Mildred from France, postmarked twelve days prior to his death.

Perhaps not his last message home but near enough, near enough...

The second is an envelope addressed to Mildred Elton Fraser, postmarked twelve days prior to his death.

Before ... for postage frank ... for new enough ... clear enough ...

CHAPTER 5

'HOODOO' KINROSS, VC: THE PRIDE OF LOUGHEED

NOT far from Courcelette on the Somme where John Lauder met his untimely end in December, 1916, a somewhat more flamboyant character had been wounded two months before. Unlike Lauder, Cecil John Kinross recovered from his injuries and would go on to win the British Empire's supreme award for gallantry, the Victoria Cross, one year later. The site of Kinross's medal winning actions was not on the Somme, however, but some 130 miles to the northeast near the Belgian village of Passchendaele.

Passchendaele! The name still has the ability to

evoke images of mud, carnage and, above all, the ultimate tragedy of the Great War. Of any war, perhaps.

Hard to believe for the present day visitor, especially on a sunny spring morning when this photo was taken, looking up the slope to the rebuilt village church from the Canadian Memorial at what was once Crest Farm. What is now a quiet street of neat houses was, in 1917, a morass at the top of which were the German positions on Passchendaele Ridge. It was through that swamp and up that slope that the Canadian infantry doggedly attacked this vital strongpoint in late October. Among the Canadian assault troops were the men of the Loyal Edmonton Regiment, known affectionately back home in Alberta as the Loyal Eddies. It was in their ranks that Cecil John Kinross served, in his own inimitable fashion, as part of the 49th Battalion which was made up mainly of those men who had volunteered so readily in January, 1915.

When Britain declared war on Germany in August, 1914, an unprecedented torrent of men eager to join up engulfed recruiting offices both at home and throughout the Empire. Nowhere was this enthusiasm more evident than in Edmonton, Alberta. It is perhaps difficult for us today to comprehend such patriotic fervour erupting in a city on the Canadian prairies some 5000 miles away from the scene of hostilities but the following three factors might help us to understand this stampede to wear the King's uniform.

First, Canada considered herself, rightly, to be a vital part of the British Empire and was therefore anxious to show the mother country just how well one of her children could do when called upon.

Secondly, in the first decade of the twentieth century, a huge wave of immigrants had arrived in Alberta with the construction of the transcontinental railroads. The vast majority came from Britain, farmers in the main who had been suffering under the agrarian slump at home. Ironically this had been caused largely by the opening up of the Canadian prairies with the subsequent availability of produce, especially wheat, at prices and in quantities with which the ordinary British farmer could not compete. So, on the basis of "If you can't beat them, join them", thousands of farming families left Britain attracted by the twin lures of cheap land and the promise of a brighter future. Although these new arrivals had been forced out of their homeland as economic migrants, most nonetheless brought with them an intense loyalty to the Crown which had been carefully implanted by school geography lessons concentrating on the pink areas of the globe. Thus, when the call came, it is not surprising that these recently displaced Britishers answered it with enthusiasm.

Finally, and perhaps most significant, was the role of the charismatic William 'Billy' Griesbach. Born in 1878, Griesbach, whose father had been an inspector in the North West Mounted Police, was deeply interested in military affairs. Prior to 1914 he had been training as a lawyer when he interrupted his studies to fight for Britain in the South African War (1899-1902). Returning to Edmonton and civilian life, he distinguished himself by becoming the city's youngest mayor. It was therefore practically preordained that, when Edmonton raised its first cavalry militia (home defence) unit in 1908, Billy Griesbach became one of its officers. Rapidly rising through the hierarchy, he was appointed in late 1914 commander of Edmonton's own battalion, the 49th.

Recruiting for the 49th began on January 4, 1915, when throngs of volunteers flocked to the Victoria Avenue Armoury in Edmonton to join "Billy's Own". Demographically these 1010 officers and men present an interesting picture, with three-quarters having been born in the United Kingdom and over half having already served in the British Army. By the end of May, 1915, they were ready for anything that fate and the fortunes of war might fling at them. They left Edmonton aboard two troop trains bound for the east coast, acquiring *en route* a mascot, a coyote pup named Lestock named after the Saskatchewan town where he had been born. Though he himself was soon consigned to London Zoo, an image of Lestock was incorporated in the 1916 version of the Eddies' cap badge where he stares out from the centre of the sails of a Flemish windmill.

Arriving in England with his men, Billy Griesbach used his not inconsiderable political clout to ensure that the 49th remained a homogeneous unit, not to be broken up and used as replacements as was the common practice. He also obtained an additional four machine guns for his battalion, making eight in total, by the simple expedient of appealing to the generosity of the citizens of Edmonton.

In October 1915, the 49th crossed the English Channel, still with their distinct identity intact as part of Princess Patricia's Canadian Light Infantry. The five months until March 1916 were spent in a support role, bringing up supplies, improving defences and generally helping to hold the line in Flanders. However, in the early spring of 1916 all this was about to change when the 49th earned its first battle honour driving the Germans from Mount Sorrell near Ypres. It was in this engagement that the battalion sustained its first serious casualties, a figure that would continue to grow over the next two years. From Belgium the 49th travelled to the Somme region of France arriving in time for that particular bloodbath in the summer of 1916 and then gradually moving north to take part in the now legendary Canadian assault on Vimy Ridge in a snowstorm on Easter Monday, 1917. Established by then as a hard, totally reliable fighting unit, the 49th was returned to Belgium to take up what turned out to be a pivotal role in the Third Battle of Ypres, known forever after as Passchendaele. And it is here that we encounter that courageous enigma, Private Cecil John Kinross, VC.

Cecil, though a member of the Canadian Expeditionary Force (CEF), was not Canadian by birth; in fact he had arrived on the prairies of Alberta just two years before the war began. So where had he been previously and why had he come to Canada? Perhaps the best way to answer these questions is to look at his family background, especially the career of his father whose strong streak of enterprise and adventure seems to have been inherited by his son.

James Stirling Kinross was born in Scotland on December 8, 1864, at the family farm near Braco, a small village in Perthshire. The nearest big town is Stirling, rather appropriate, given James' middle name. Gannochan Farm was a substantial holding of 258 acres and had been in the Kinross family for three generations. According to the 1851 Census it was able to provide a living for the family and up to ten labourers. Today the farm is deserted, the almost fortress-like steading deteriorating while the house, with its peeling

Gannochan Farm

wallpaper and broken windows, bears mute testimony to its former existence as a family home. Surrounded by sheep grazing peacefully, the building's only inhabitants today are pigeons, bats and the occasional gentleman of the road. And possibly a shadow or two from its past lurking in dusty corners.

Despite the apparent viability of the property, James left his home as a teenager to seek his fortune in the New World. Yet his first transatlantic adventure did not lead him to Canada where he and his family would settle years later, but to the wide open spaces of Texas. There he became a cowboy working on the huge King Ranch which was so vast that it would have constituted a fair sized county back home in Scotland. Nothing daunted, James seems to have adapted well to his new environment.

According to Kinross family history, James was deputised into the Texas Rangers, was present at the capture of the Apache chief, Geronimo, and made the acquaintance of Doc Holliday of OK Corral notoriety. It is tempting to speculate that some at least of his father's derring-do and facility with firearms was passed down to Cecil, who would use them later to great effect not on the rolling grasslands of North America, but in a muddy field in Belgium.

However, James' exciting life in Texas was not to last. In 1888 he returned to Britain at the request of his brother, John, who had moved to a farm at Hurley in Warwickshire in the English Midlands. The name of this farm was Flanders Hall, an eerie portent of Cecil's future when one considers that the most significant incident in his life would take place in that very region of northern Belgium. Having been given the tenancy of the farm by John, James was financially secure enough to marry a local girl, Emily Hull, in 1891. Cecil, the middle one of their five children, was born in 1896 in the south of England at Dews Farm, Uxbridge, Middlesex, to which the family had moved as part of their constant search to better their economic circumstances. By 1904, however, the family had returned to Emily's home area in Warwickshire and it was there that Cecil received much of his senior education at the locally well regarded Coleshill Grammar School. Having graduated at age fifteen, Cecil's post-school career in England was not to last long. In 1912 the family, under the guidance of the intrepid James, was on the move once more. This time it was the big one, emigration to Canada. At last James had spotted a real window of opportunity, the promised land of Alberta, where the family settled on farmland near the little township of Lougheed.

Lougheed had been established just one year prior to the arrival of the Kinross family with the construction of the Canadian Pacific Railroad; appropriately the first building had been the station. The township lay on the south side of the Iron River Valley about 90 miles east of Edmonton surrounded by vast tracts of rolling countryside eminently suitable for growing the cereal crops that so attracted the incoming farming families. As they prospered, so the settlement grew into the very pleasant small town of some 230 souls which it is today. Though the Kinross family firmly intended to stay and succeed in Lougheed, Cecil himself was not going to be able to put down permanent roots there for some time. Within two and a half years of his arrival he became increasingly aware of Kitchener's siren call to the young men of the Empire to come "home" to defend the mother country. This was an appeal that Cecil John Kinross was not about to ignore.

Cecil was inducted into the army at Calgary on 21 October, 1915. His enlistment papers tell us that he was just half an inch below six feet in height, of strong physique with dark brown hair and a religious affiliation to the Church of England. His eyes, which are the most arresting feature of the photos which exist of him in the army, are noted merely as being "blue" though they might well have merited an additional comment such as "piercing".

By the end of 1915 Cecil was considered proficient enough to be let loose on the Germans and so, on December 18, he embarked with the 51st Battalion of the CEF aboard the S.S. Missanbie for the UK. After three months further training in England, Cecil once more boarded ship to cross the Channel on 16 March, 1916, for his first taste of combat. By this time, however, he was no longer a member of the 51st. Instead he had been transferred and was now a part of the 49th Battalion, the Loyal Eddies.

Back Row: J. Barton, A. Bonnin, Lynn Disturnal, A. Dash, P. Rose
Middle Row: W. Cookson, Unknown, W. Guthrie, C. Kinross, J. Liddle, J. Muirhead
Bottom Row: W. MacLaren, P. Watson, W. Holdsworth, Fisher, R. Kenny, A. Nicol, Unknown

51st Battalion Canadian Over-seas Expeditionary Force, Edmonton Alberta
*all men from Lougheed & Sedgewick Area except Fisher

Cecil: Third from the right, middle row

From March to August, 1916, Cecil fought with the Eddies round Ypres in Belgium and then moved south to the Somme in France where his luck, such as it was, temporarily ran out. In early October, 1916, he sustained shrapnel wounds to his right arm and ribs which kept him sidelined until November 6 of the same year. After further action on the Somme and at Vimy Ridge in the early months of 1917, Cecil and the 49th moved gradually northwards, returning in October to their old stamping ground, the dreaded Ypres Salient. It was there at Furst Farm, near what remained of the little village of Passchendaele, that Cecil John Kinross was to have his date with destiny.

At first glance Cecil was perhaps unlikely material for a military hero. Certainly he looked the part with a warrior's physique and a bold countenance dominated by those eyes. In addition to these attributes, Cecil also bore the scars of battle that he had earned down on the Somme. However, if his conduct was anything to go by, he might have been looked on as more promising material for the awkward squad.

Known as "Hoodoo" to his fellow soldiers, Cecil is described unsparingly in the history of the Loyal Eddies, *A City Goes to War*, as:

> "...A thoroughly unorthodox soldier......the kind of soldier who perpetually flirted with court martial..."

One of his officers gives us what is, as near as dammit, the definitive picture of this maverick:

> "Of the multifarious characters the Forty-Ninth boasted – and there were many – one of the strangest if not the kingpin of them

all was "Hoodoo" Kinross. No officer whose runner he became ever got any change out of him. He was one of the most *'c'est la guerre, ce n'est fait rien'* guys that I have ever come up against. He was strictly a front line soldier and gloried to be there, but he loathed parades. When he was forced to parade, whether in reserve or at rest, his appearance was usually disgraceful. There would be a hard look in his eyes during rebuke, almost but not quite enough to put him on a charge of unspoken insolence. He was regarded, frankly, when in back areas, as incorrigible."

However, as this same officer reveals, it was only in "back areas" that this "incorrigible" attitude was in evidence, not in the front line, especially when the going got tough. There Cecil's truculence became a positive virtue. And the going had certainly become very tough by October 30, 1917, when the Eddies found themselves bogged down at Furst Farm, near Passchendaele. There, as cliché has it, "Cometh the hour, cometh the man".

The situation and Cecil's response to it is probably best summed up by quoting his "gazetting". (This term refers to the custom of bravery awards being first announced in the *London Gazette*, the official journal of the British Government.) On January 11, 1918, readers were treated to the following:

"For most conspicuous bravery in action during prolonged and severe operations. Shortly after the attack was launched, the company to which he belonged came under intense artillery fire and further advance was held up by very heavy fire from an enemy machine-gun. Private Kinross, making a careful survey of the situation, deliberately divested himself of all his equipment save his rifle and bandolier and, regardless of his personal safety, advanced alone over open ground in broad daylight, charged the enemy machine-gun, killing the crew of six and seized and destroyed the gun. His superb example and courage instilled the greatest confidence in his company and enabled a further advance of 300 yards to be made and a highly important position to be established. Throughout the day he showed marvellous coolness and courage, fighting with the utmost aggressiveness against heavy odds until seriously wounded."

Gazetted descriptions are notoriously short on details of geography and time but, from this one, several points can be gleaned. First, Cecil's action was only the culmination of his front line activities. It would appear that he had been annoying the Germans for some considerable time. Second, Cecil's one man war was not a spur of the moment impulse. Instead he had carefully and deliberately sized up the situation and the best way to go about resolving it. As reported in *The Times History of the War*, "No other VC had indicated quite the same cool, deliberate preparation for a final effort as this stripping to the bandolier and rifle". Third, it would seem

Furst Farm today

that Cecil positively enjoyed combat, else why would he have continued to fight on at Furst Farm, desisting only when forced to do so by severe wounds? It appears that "Hoodoo" Kinross, individualist nonpareil, was just the man the 49th needed, perhaps not on the parade ground but quite definitely in the thick of battle.

Further, more personal, information can be obtained from Bob Gilmour's article "Victoria Cross Symbolizes the Legend of Kinross" (*Edmonton Journal*, April 1, 1989). Described as "a farmer soldier from Lougheed" and also as "devil-may-care", Cecil is revealed at Furst Farm as, typically, flouting army convention once again. This time, however, it was not what he perceived as needless bull that Cecil was ignoring but the time-honoured old sweats' advice never to volunteer for anything. Yet this is precisely what Cecil did when he found Company B had been brought to a standstill. The article further indicates that the result of Cecil's heroism gave encouragement not only to his immediate companions but to all Canadians at the front. Dr C.D. McBride of Edmonton, who was in 1917 a stretcher-bearer in another division, told Bob how Cecil's action was generally regarded as that of "...a wild Canadian running amok trying to defeat the whole German Army single-handed..." with the result that "...all of us from Alberta puffed out our chests with pride in this man".

Cecil's actions evidently contributed greatly to the troops' morale, a psychological factor that was going to be so necessary in the final push up the slope to the blighted ruins of Passchendaele village. It eventually fell to the Canadians on November 10 and 11, 1917 but ironically, was retaken by the Germans the following year in their spring blitzkrieg. As Nigel Cage puts it in *Passchendaele: The Fight for the Village*:

> "Passchendaele fell rapidly to the Germans in their Lys offensive, launched in April 1918, bringing bitter recriminations from many Canadians at the wasteful loss of life for a position that was lost within minutes. The Canadians had 15,654 casualties for their month or so on the Passchendaele front... Passchendaele did not see British arms again, for it was... Belgian troops that finally liberated the red brick stained mud that had been Passchendaele in September 1918."

However, the heroism of Cecil and his comrades had not been in vain. Their efforts, admittedly at horrendous cost, had further weakened the German Army and had provided temporary respite for Ypres, the linchpin of the Salient and symbol to the British of their ability to survive and, ultimately, to prevail.

Cecil's immediate future following his VC action was dictated by his physical state. Badly wounded in the head and left arm by a shell burst, he ended up in the Canadian Hospital at Orpington in England where he was told in January, 1918, that he had won the VC, which was pinned to his uniform by King George V at Buckingham Palace in March of the same year.

Of course, Cecil being Cecil, there was a hitch waiting just around the corner. Two hours after his audience with the King, when he was about to board a train to visit relatives in Scotland, Cecil was arrested by military police for fraudulently wearing the VC ribbon. Probably with a great deal of satisfaction, aware as we are of his attitude towards authority, Cecil was able to prove his right to wear the medal by showing the colonel in charge the Cross itself with the Kinross name engraved on the back.

Posted to the 21st Reserve Battalion, Cecil remained in Britain until January, 1919, when he sailed home to Canada. On receipt of his honourable discharge from the Canadian Army on 17 February, Cecil returned to Lougheed. From there he was invited to the Pantages Theatre in Edmonton for a civic reception packed to overflowing by wildly appreciative citizens. At this venue the Mayor presented Cecil with a purse of gold.

But this was not to be the only mark of esteem to come Cecil's way. Shortly after his homecoming the Canadian government granted him 160 acres of prime farm land eight miles west of Lougheed. Then, in 1929, Cecil returned to the UK at the invitation of the Prince of Wales for the British Legion dinner in London to honour the recipients of the Empire's premier military award. In 1939 he was presented to King George VI and Queen Elizabeth on their Canadian tour while, in 1956, he was back in the British capital to meet Queen Elizabeth II at the VC Centenary Review in Hyde Park. Feted everywhere they went, Cecil and his fellow Canadian VCs were treated as the heroes they undoubtedly were. Cecil obviously enjoyed this last expedition immensely, describing it as "wonderful", which was a nice touch, coming as it did just a year before his untimely death. It also gave Cecil a chance to renew his acquaintance both with English beer and a fellow Loyal Eddy VC, John Chipman Kerr, who had won his decoration on the Somme in 1916. *A City Goes to War* tells us that "Kerr and Kinross became 'Chip' and 'Hoodoo' once more when they journeyed to Liphook to belly up to the bar in the Red Lion".

J. Kerr, V.C., Lougheed, Alta., being presented to His Majesty on the steps of the Legislative Bldg., at Edmonton on June 2nd, 1939.

The Lougheed Hotel

Perhaps for Cecil the most satisfying social engagements of his post-army days were the Annual Dinners held by the Regimental Association. One can easily imagine Cecil in his element at the 1929 soiree which is described in the regimental history as "...a mopping-up party in which discipline was entirely lacking..." Further evidence from the same source reveals that "the great rallying of the clan" in 1933 at which Cecil was the guest of honour was "a lively full-blooded occasion". Not surprisingly, Cecil was an enthusiastic participant in these yearly celebrations where he could meet up with his old buddies and generally have a good time. Perhaps the real significance of these veterans' reunions was best expressed at the 1929 event by the organiser, Colonel Weaver, when he stated that "No bond, except that of matrimony, is as strong in our lives as having served in the 49th in a World War".

Arguably the greatest honour bestowed on Cecil came in 1951 when Mount Kinross in Jasper National Park, Alberta, was given his family name.

Sadly, not even VC heroes can defy the Grim Reaper indefinitely. On June 21, 1957, Cecil died, alone, in a room in the Lougheed Hotel where he had lived on his Army pension since his retiral from farming.

"Hoodoo" Kinross VC, that one-time flirter with insubordination, was buried with full military honours on the prairie which had become his home. The ceremony was attended by hundreds of his fellow Albertans among whom were many of the Loyal Eddies of the Great War. One of his pall-bearers was Corporal Alex Brereton, another Albertan VC, who had, like Cecil, won his medal by taking out a troublesome machine-gun post.

Two final honours remained. The children's playground in Lougheed was named after the old warrior, something that would have appealed to him greatly, as was the local branch of the Canadian Legion.

A special plaque was dedicated there in 1995, eighty years after he had gone to war.

Cecil: Some Personal Glimpses

What kind of man was Cecil John Kinross? To try to come to some sort of consensus, let's look at comments made about him by people who either knew him personally or know of him through tales handed down from an older generation.

After interviewing many people in the Lougheed and Edmonton areas for his 1989 *Edmonton Journal* article referred to earlier, Bob Gilmour felt able to describe Cecil as "cheerful, unassuming and everybody's friend".

Not a bad epitaph and a good place to begin this selection of reminiscences.

Denise Sigalet, a long-time resident of Lougheed, offers some tantalising insights based on conversations with fellow residents with personal links to Cecil. She suggests that, for Cecil, personal possessions didn't come top of the list of his priorities:

"It's my understanding that Cecil never did farm his own land. He must have rented it out, as the story goes that he preferred to work for the other farmers around Lougheed. I've been told that he was a very hard worker but also played hard and pulled a few stunts now and then."

Jim Wright, a close friend of Denise, reveals Cecil's natural modesty and also his kindness and sense of fun, especially involving children with whom he got on well.

"I was a child when Cecil worked for my father on the farm. Cecil would never talk about how he won the VC. Instead he would make up some colourful story that didn't depict himself as the hero!"

In the same vein Denise adds,

"For children, Cecil would make up a fantastic story rather than the REAL fantastic story! I don't think he was one to talk about himself but would not want to brush the kids off."

This is not to say that Cecil wasn't proud of winning the VC; his eagerness to travel to the Royal occasions in England indicates otherwise. But, like many winners of the honour, he chose rarely, if ever, to talk about what he had achieved.

Though he seems to have had a very good way with children, Cecil never married. Denise guesses that the reason for his bachelor life is that "he was too busy being wild and crazy to ever settle down... a man who had done and seen the things that he had would have had trouble settling down to the everyday routine of life".

However, though he lacked wife and family, it's doubtful that the gregarious Cecil was lonely with, as Denise points out, "a second home at the hotel and the Legion."

As for being "wild and crazy", Cecil seems to have lived up to that description long after the events at Furst Farm. His fellow survivors from the Loyal Eddies were certainly convinced that Cecil was no ordinary mortal. Bob Gilmour cites two examples supplied by Cecil's old soldier pals which reveal his rather unique take on life. In 1934, prior to a tonsillectomy, he refused an anaesthetic, an action almost incomprehensible to us today but possibly a result of a dislike of chloroform acquired during his wartime hospitalisations. Then, at a later date, on a bitterly cold Lougheed day, he peeled off his coat and plunged through a hole cut in the ice of a stream. He took this rather extreme course of action in order to settle, entirely to his own satisfaction, an argument with a friend about whether it took more courage to win a VC or to dive into the freezing water. Not only does this episode remind us of Cecil in 1917 "divesting himself of equipment" before conclusively settling another much more serious dispute, but it also provides us with a great example of one of Cecil's legendary "stunts" and his eccentric sense of humour.

Jim Wright gives us similar glimpses of Cecil:

"I remember CJ coming to our place in 1956, just before he left for his audience with the Queen. We were all very excited for him.

Much was being made locally of his trip since trips to the old country were a very big deal at the time. He had a large white Stetson which he swore he was going to wear when he met Her Majesty. I have no knowledge of whether he actually did wear the hat before the Queen but I bet he did on every other occasion he could get away with it. Neither do I know where the hat came from. I think he was being feted quite a bit at the time and was enjoying the notoriety."

Jim also recalls that his mother had a plate which had fleetingly belonged to Cecil:

"He won it in a draw during a dance in the Lougheed Community Hall. As he was dancing around the Hall with the plate in one hand over his head, he spun by my mother and passed her the plate, saying 'Here, lassie, this is yours.' My mother had many memories of CJ. Being quite a party animal he went to all the dances and social occasions."

Tom Barton, one of Bob Gilmour's interviewees, knew Cecil well and, indeed, at the time of the article (1989) actually farmed Cecil's land.

"Cecil was really well liked around Lougheed. He was a happy-go-lucky guy and full of fun. You couldn't get him to talk about the VC or what happened. He was a very proud man. He didn't give a damn for anything."

Perhaps Tom's last sentence, "He didn't give a damn for anything", says it all. Cecil seems to have been one of those extraordinary people who was able to live life to the full with absolutely no regrets and yet endear himself to those whose lives they touch along the way. The kind of man, in fact, who was always ready to take whatever steps were necessary to settle a point, whether they were across a muddy field in Flanders to an enemy machine-gun post or to a hole in the ice on a biting winter's day in Alberta.

Appropriately the last word, for now at least, should be left to Denise Sigalet who has done so much to keep alive the memory of Lougheed's veterans:

"I am guessing that Cecil lived the remainder of his life precisely the way he wanted to. The stories round here tell of a 'character' who enjoyed his beer and wasn't one to conform to what society approved of. Yes, sadly, he died alone in his hotel room, possibly after a night at the pub, but given a choice of when and where he wanted to go, he might well have chosen that very place."

Though many years have passed since Cecil's demise, interest in him remains strong in Canada. In recent years the former base of the Loyal Eddies in Edmonton has been redeveloped as a civilian housing estate. One of the new streets is Kinross Road, complete with a plaque explaining the significance of the name.

I wish I could end there as it seems so appropriate but, as ever, there's a little bit more to come about Cecil – the twin "mysteries" of his birth and the "Hoodoo" nickname.

Over the years a misconception as to the place and date of Cecil's birth has grown until it has become practically the authorised version. I first became aware of this upon reading an article in the files of our local paper, the *Alloa Advertiser*. There Cecil was identified as one of Clackmannanshire's five VCs. Nice to contemplate but, unfortunately, untrue.

In the late David Harvey's wonderful two-volume work on the holders of the VC, *Monuments to Courage*, Cecil's date of birth is given as "probably" 13 July, 1897, with the caveat of "although attested 17 February, 1895". In addition to this, his birthplace is given as Hillend Farm, Clackmannan. Both of these pieces of information are wrong.

Further confusion arises when the renowned Canon Lummis Archive of VC Recipients held by the Imperial War Museum, London, is consulted. Here Cecil's birth date is stated to be 17 February, 1896, the same day as that contained in Harvey's caveat but a year later. The location of Cecil's birthplace agrees with Harvey as being Clackmannan but the possibility of it being Stirling is also raised. Lummis' research was reasonably thorough. By contacting the Registrar General of Scotland, he was able to prove that no male by the name of Kinross had been born in Scotland in either 1895 or 1896. Nevertheless, the good Canon had got his ecclesiastical knickers in a right old twist with regard to Cecil's origins and, just to muddy the waters further, he discovered that a John Kinross had indeed been born at Hillend Farm, Clackmannan, in 1897. Lummis had given birth to a myth which later writers, like the estimable Mr Harvey repeated.

It is an indisputable fact that there was indeed a Kinross family in Hillend Farm, Clackmannan, in 1897 and a son named John was born there in that year. But he was not our Cecil John. He was his cousin. Donald Kinross, Hillend John's father, had left Gannochan Farm, Braco, like his older brother James, Cecil's father. However, Donald had travelled only twenty miles from home to the quiet pastures round Clackmannan, not to the wilds of Texas. Interestingly, later in life, this John Kinross, like his cousin Cecil, also emigrated to Canada.

The Kinross family has quite definitely identified Cecil's birthplace as Dews Farm, Harefield, Uxbridge, Middlesex in the south of England, where the birth was registered in March, 1896 (Document GO12218). The date of birth is also clarified by this certificate as being 17 February, 1896.

The belief, alluded to in the Lummis Archive, that the town of Stirling in Scotland was Cecil's birthplace, seems to have arisen from the fact that someone unknown crossed out the correct information, 'Uxbridge', on Cecil's attestation paper for the Canadian Army, and substituted 'Stirling'. Why this was done and by whom is lost in mists of time and is probably best left there as it is demonstrably false.

Of course, Cecil himself is partly to blame for any doubts about his real age as he gave his date of birth as 17 February, 1895, on this same attestation paper and his age on his grave marker is shown as 62. It is possible that Cecil in his inimitably cavalier manner deliberately gave a wrong birth date in order to make himself appear older, perhaps because age affected when a soldier could serve overseas or, more importantly, receive the rum ration.

One interesting point which emerged during my research is that English-born Cecil seems to have taken great pride in his Scottish ancestry even though his only visit to the land of his father was his post-decoration adventure in 1918. It's tempting to believe that Cecil's undoubted "thrawnness" (Scots for "stubbornness"), his dislike of, even contempt for, authority, his strong streak of wildness and his love of what Scots refer to as "nonsense", came from his Scottish genes.

Now we come to a final matter which needs clearing up – why was Cecil nicknamed "Hoodoo" Kinross?

Both David Haas, the Curator of the Loyal Edmonton Military Museum, and Denise Sigalet of Lougheed, agree in their speculation, put forward totally independent of each other, about the origin of "Hoodoo". David states that, in Alberta, hoodoos are "eerie, eroded wind formations in the Drumheller Badlands", while Denise describes them as "tall, pedestal-type sedimentary formations with flat tops, carved by glaciers in the Ice Age".

Using this information one might just see Cecil as a rock, tall and battered but still standing, despite numerous attempts by the military authorities to erode his sense of his own worth and to make him conform.

However, David brings an additional theory to our attention. "Hoodoo" can also mean "a malevolent supernatural force, a hex". Remember the description in *A City Goes to War* of Cecil having "a hard look in his eyes"? Some poor officer being stared down by "Hoodoo" Kinross might well have felt that he'd had the evil eye put on him! Or might it simply be that Cecil got himself in so many scrapes in the Army that he felt that he was jinxed, while others might have taken a more objective view of his troubles?

No matter, it all adds colour to the legend of Cecil, the Hoodoo from Lougheed.

* * *

Postscript

On November 30, 2011, I received a most welcome communication from Jennifer Kolthammer, the wife of Brian Kolthammer, the great-nephew of Cecil John Kinross, VC, as a result of which I visited the Canadian Military Archives where his service record has been put online. Once again the question of Hoodoo's date of birth raises its head. It appears ten times as 17 February, 1895, once as 17 January, 1895, and once as 1897! Despite all this information to the contrary, I shall stick with 17 February, 1896, the date shown on the form registering his birth (Document GO12218, dated March, 1896, and held in the National Archives at Kew, London). Not only is this the date accepted by the Kinross family but it

was confirmed as recently as 17 February, 2011, when the Deputy High Commissioner for Canada unveiled a Blue Plaque commemorating Cecil at his birthplace, Dews Farm in Harefield, Middlesex. The plaque quite unequivocally states the date of birth as 17 February, 1896, and to clear up another misconception, Harefield is part of Uxbridge, not Oxbridge, as is frequently stated on Cecil's military record.

However, the most interesting discovery in these Canadian documents is the revelation of the extent of the wounds suffered by Cecil during his VC action. The after-effects of his injuries might well go a long way to explaining his subsequent postwar behaviour. He was left with a 50% loss of power in his left hand and forearm which made it difficult for him "to use farm implements such as a fork or spade". In addition, this arm became very cold and numb in inclement weather which would have been an obvious disadvantage during the prairie winters back in Alberta. Indeed, "partial paralysis" of the limb is mentioned. It seems more than likely that this is why he didn't go back to working the land granted to him by the Canadian Government, renting it out instead and taking on light work for his neighbours.

His gallantry also left him with a history of headaches which occurred frequently and lasted for two or three days. How severe these were is not indicated but they must have been debilitating enough to be officially mentioned. Perhaps this is why he never married, preferring to be alone with his pain. For Cecil, as with so many other survivors of the Great War, the conflict didn't end in 1918 but continued to haunt him until his death 39 years later.

CHAPTER 6

A WALK ACROSS THE ANCRE

I T'S early September on the Thiepval ridge and, in the middle distance, the mid-morning sun is burning off the last vestiges of the mist rising from the flat bottom land of the River Ancre and the fields beyond. There's that golden sheen to the Somme countryside as if summer's not yet ready to bid farewell, and the farmers are busy in the fields. From where I'm standing under the arch of the immense Memorial to the Missing of the Somme, I can see Ulster Tower and, about two kilometres further on, the trees at Newfoundland Park where we shall shortly be bound.

The memorial, Sir Edwin Lutyen's masterwork, stands on part of the Leipzig Redoubt, a German fortification before which so many Allied soldiers fell in 1916. Dominating the countryside for miles around, its redbrick immensity never fails to inspire a true sense of awe. Unveiled in 1932, the Monument lists on its white limestone panels the names of over 73,000 men of Britain and her Empire who never came home and yet have "No Known Grave". Many of the missing commemorated here do indeed have marked graves

Memorial to the Missing of the Somme at Thiepval

somewhere on the Somme, only we don't know which one of those headstones inscribed "Known Unto God" belongs to them. The remainder still lie, as yet undiscovered, beneath the surrounding fields or have vanished completely and forever, testament to the terrible power of the high explosive shell.

Paul Reed, in his excellent *Walking the Somme*, manages to provide a sense of who these missing are, or were. The vast crowd of pilgrims at the unveiling of the Memorial in 1932 knew. They were there to remember "husbands, fathers, sons, brothers, cousins, and, no doubt, lovers", not just to look at the names on the panels, important though those were. Just by being there and remembering, went, I suppose, some of the way towards humanising the unimaginable inhumanity of what had happened here.

On this particular occasion I'm alone but I'm not lonely. The names are here for company. It's too early for the school parties, earnest teachers and well-primed kids with clipboards at the ready. Once upon a time I was one of those teachers and even now, years later, youthful faces from my past return and I'm glad I knew them. Where are they all now, those with whom I shared those great adventures?

The walk down the road from the Thiepval Memorial to Ulster Tower is a delight on a day like this. The only sound is the buzzing of the bees as they forage for pollen in the steep banks covered with wild flowers. Occasionally a car passes and sometimes a moped. But they're soon gone and peace descends once more, making it well-nigh impossible to grasp that it was from this very road that part of the attack on the disastrous first day of the Somme began. On my left as I progress towards the Tower is Connaught Cemetery which contains 1278 graves and perhaps the finest yew hedge I've ever seen, courtesy of the gardeners of the Commonwealth War Graves Commission. Across the road and up the slope is Mill Road Cemetery where the headstones lie flat on the sward due to the very uncertain nature of the surface caused by the network of German tunnels in the chalk below. Both cemeteries testify to the horrific losses suffered on July 1 by the men of the 36th (Ulster) Division who, by the end of that bloody day, were, in cricketing terms, approximately five thousand for four – five thousand casualties for four VCs, that is.

In their *Battlefield Guide to the Somme*, Tonie and Valmai Holt sum up the Division's achievement and sacrifice far better than I:

"The Ulsters walked, then charged, from the forward edge of Thiepval Wood, past where

95

the Tower stands and on to the crest and beyond. They were the only soldiers north of the Albert-Bapaume Road to pierce the German lines... Some say their achievement was due to a mixture of Irish individualism, alcoholic bravura and religious fervour... It was also the emotive anniversary of the Battle of the Boyne by the Old Calendar. Whatever the reason, it was a magnificent feat of arms... If the rest of the 4th Army had advanced at the same speed it is certain that the outcome would have been totally different."

Just a short distance up the road stands Ulster Tower. Opened at the end of 1921, the Tower is a replica of Helen's Tower on the Clandeboye Estate in Northern Ireland where the 36th trained before shipping out to France. It was built to commemorate the sacrifice of these men of Ulster, many of whom were members of the Orange Order. Which brings us to the thorny question of sectarianism and the Northern Irish Question. Up until the 1990s the Tower was not just a memorial but also a significant gathering point for the Loyal Orange Order (LOL). Matters came to a head

when the Order dedicated a black marble obelisk, specifically to commemorate the LOL soldiers, this at a time when efforts to bring together the two warring factions in Northern Island were gaining momentum. The siting of this "unofficial" memorial at the entrance to the Tower grounds in 1993 caused quite a stir both locally and in Northern Ireland. In response, the Somme Association was formed in 1994 in Belfast "to provide a basis for the two traditions in Northern Ireland to come together and learn of their common heritage", a fair decision since many a Catholic lad from the Province had died for Britain beside their Protestant fellow countrymen in the fields round about. The "controversial" memorial was then discreetly positioned round the back of the Tower, where those who wish can pay their respects in private, and the Somme Association undertook to care for the Tower as Northern Ireland's National Memorial, regardless of religion.

I must admit that, when I first visited the Tower many years ago, I felt intimidated by the very oppressive sense of exclusivity that prevailed. Now, there's a warm welcome and cups of tea courtesy of the Ulster curators. They care for the Tower for nine months of the year, returning to Northern Ireland for the festive season and beyond, but, come each spring, they're back dispensing their own particular brand of sunshine.

When you visit, leave enough time to visit Thiepval Wood, a short distance back down the road to the rear of Connaught Cemetery. The Wood, from the edge of which the Ulstermen advanced on July 1, is now owned by the Somme Association. Due to its archaeological sensitivity and also for reasons of safety, it's strictly off limits to the casual visitor but everyone's welcome on the tours run by the occupants of the Tower.

Close by the excavated trenches in the Wood stands a simple wooden cross marking the site of an action by a young Ulsterman on the First of July, 1916, for which he was awarded one of the four VCs earned by the 36th (Ulster) Division on that day. When two live grenades fell into a crowded trench, Private Billy McFadzean reacted immediately and fatally. As his VC citation states, "Private McFadzean... with heroic courage threw himself on top of the bombs which exploded, blowing him to pieces... he gave his life for his comrades".

His name is back there, up the slope at Thiepval, and we know where and how he died. It's just that there was nothing much left of him to bury and no time, anyway, to dig a grave.

Leaving the Tower with a promise to look in again "next year", it's off down the road to the once bloody River Ancre of dread reputation.

Again a memory from a bygone trip thrusts itself upon me. This time the image is of a wiry Frenchman in Tour de France gear and cap, astride a fine racer, cycling ahead of our bus, head down and going strongly – with the smoke from his Gauloise streaming out behind him.

Nearly at the bottom of the hill now, and at the edge of a field on my left I espy a French family having a picnic. Sitting in the shade of a leafy willow, they're tucking into what looks like a very civilised lunch – cheese, sausage, fruit and the inevitable batons of bread, washed down, no doubt, by the equally inevitable *vin rouge*. A friendly exchange of waves and then on to the bridge over the Ancre. Ah, the River Ancre...

Today the water is running crystal clear over the green tresses of weed which billow out along the river's bed. Back in November, 1916 this same river and its surrounds had been reduced by constant shelling to one vast, hellish sea of glutinous, yellow mud. Many of the men, both British and German, who fought here were reduced to despair by their constant battle, not just against the enemy, but also against this greater opponent, described by Nigel Cave as "a vile swamp" in which "communications became impossible". Some troops cracked completely and, as I stand on the bridge gazing into the trout-rich water, the name of one of those poor souls comes to me – Sub-Lieutenant Edwin Leopold Arthur Dyett of the Nelson Battalion, Royal Naval Division (RND).

The full details of Dyett's "offence" and subsequent trial can be accessed through the books of Judge Anthony Babington, Messrs. Putkowski and Sykes and, especially, Leonard Sellers, all of which are listed in the bibliography for this chapter. Using the information I have gleaned from these sources I shall attempt to give you a summary, short but I hope fair, of the case and its repercussions.

Born into a family with a very distinguished maritime background, Dyett had enlisted at age 19 in the Royal Naval Volunteer Reserve (RNVR) in 1915, expecting, not unreasonably, to follow in the sea-booted steps of his father for a life on the ocean wave. Unfortunately this particular ambition was to remain unfulfilled. Due to the horrendous losses sustained by the British Army at Gallipoli and on the Western Front, Dyett was deployed as a land-based sailor as part of the Royal Naval Division. In other words, he was ordered to become a soldier, a role for which, as we shall see, he was singularly unsuited. Who knows, Dyett might well have had a long and honourable career on the briny if the enthusiasm he had shown while on his initial naval training had been allowed to mature. But this was not to be. Instead Dyett, along with his fellow "sailors" in the RND, was sent off to the valley of the Ancre in November, 1916. Well aware of his own deficiencies, Dyett had previously applied for transfer to sea duty on the grounds that his nerves couldn't

take the strain of trench warfare for which he hadn't signed up in the first place. His C.O. also recognised his shortcomings and protected him as much as possible until dire necessity intervened and Dyett's presence on the battlefield was called upon. By the time he was given the order to proceed to the front line on November 13, 1916, he seems to have been past caring.

Getting as far as Beaucourt Station, not far from the front line, Dyett found the situation very confusing and declared that he was going back to Battalion HQ to clarify matters, taking with him some stragglers he'd found on the way. What exactly happened next is very difficult to ascertain, especially as no attempt was made to get testimony from any of the men who allegedly spent the night of the 13th with him in a shelter. Nothing more was heard of Dyett until the 15th when he turned up at Battalion HQ at Englebelmer as if everything was hunky-dory. Unfortunately he'd misjudged his situation rather badly. He was found guilty of the capital offence of desertion in the field largely on the testimony of a fellow officer who not only held a grudge against Dyett but was also, reputedly, generally unpopular in the Battalion.

Dyett's Grave, Le Crotoy

Edwin Dyett was shot at dawn on Friday, January 5, 1917, at St Firmin on the Channel Coast to where the RND had been sent to recover as best they could from the mauling they'd received at the Battle of the Ancre. And so the case might have been closed – but it wasn't.

We're now going to have a look at the justice, or, rather, injustice, of the execution of Dyett and, naturally, I leave myself open to the accusation of employing hindsight and applying contemporary standards to happenings which occurred many years before I was born. I acknowledge this but I have my own standard for assessing the morality of society in the past and it is this. Where there were protests over laws when they were in force and, as a result of these protests, changes were made to those laws, then those laws were indeed unjust in their own time. Slavery and factory conditions spring immediately to mind as historical institutions which were quite legal in their day but are now regarded as inhumane and morally reprehensible. In both these cases there were massive contemporary protests which eventually led Parliament both to abolish "the peculiar institution" and to bring in the Factory Acts. I rest my case.

In the immediate aftermath of the shooting, questions were raised in the House by the tenacious Ernest Thurtle, not just about Dyett but about military executions in general, a bone he would worry at throughout the 1920s. Significantly for his Parliamentary campaign, Thurtle had the additional clout of having served at the front himself before being invalided back home with a severe wound to his throat.

Dyett's father emigrated to New Zealand with his immediate family and renounced his British citizenship in disgust while the Darling Committee, as early as 1919, raised grave doubts about the lack of proper legal protection for an accused such as Dyett due to the lack of adequately qualified "prisoner's friends". Certainly the one who was meant to help poor old Edwin did him no favours.

Horatio Bottomley, publisher and embezzler, in fact the Robert Maxwell of his time, took up the case through the medium of his hugely popular *John Bull* weekly magazine and set a whole pack of terriers loose on the establishment, as he was wont to do. No matter that his reputation ended up in tatters, what he did over the Dyett Affair and other military cock-ups endeared him, for a short time at least, not only to the serving soldiers who apparently devoured each issue of his journal but also to that large segment of the general public who ate up the remaining copies. Alas, the Establishment does not forgive or forget and Horatio ultimately ended up sewing mailbags.

Perhaps the most significant reaction to Dyett's execution came from Alan Herbert, who was there on the battlefield at Beaucourt on the Ancre on November 13, 1916 as part of the self-same RND as Dyett. 'A.P.' as Herbert was later known in literary and theatrical circles and also by his adoring public, was so incensed by Dyett's mistreatment that he was moved to write *The Secret Battle* which was published in 1919. Though a commercial failure it was read by some very influential people, among them Lloyd George, Winston Churchill and the future Field Marshal Bernard Montgomery, 'Monty' himself. For the last of these three especially it provided much food for thought.

So why was Dyett executed? Probably because of the virtual impossibility of stopping the disciplinary mill of the British Army once it had been set a-grinding. Though there was a recommendation for clemency, usual in such cases and normally acted upon as Dyett himself naively believed it would be, this was ignored by the man at the top, Douglas Haig, who would appear to have had it in for the RND, "the most eccentric formation under British arms" (Cave). Dyett probably was "guilty as charged" according to the letter of military law, but he received no justice.

According to the chaplain who stayed with him right up until the last moment, Edwin died with courage and dignity. Like Cawdor in *Macbeth*, "Nothing in his life became him like the leaving it".

It would be nice to depart this sorry farrago on an optimistic note, no matter how faint, and I think I can. Edwin Dyett did not die entirely in vain. It was largely due to the furore caused by his execution and the exertions of the aforementioned Ernest Thurtle that in 1930 the Army and Air Force Act finally abolished the death penalty in the forces for desertion, cowardice and all the other demons a serving man might fall prey to under the stress of combat. A newer, slightly more humane breeze was blowing through the cobwebs in the Establishment, even though it left unruffled the scales of those Tory dinosaurs in the Lords who tried with all their might to block Thurtle's reform.

Back to the present. The sun breaks through the clouds which had crept across it and the Ancre flows cheerily onward to Albert and the Somme. The warmth returns and the sound of the water reminds me that I could do with a drink. As I recall, there's a frites shack near Newfoundland Park so it's over the railway line, through Hamel village and up the winding road past the communal cemetery towards the treeline on the ridge.

Newfoundland Park is the main memorial in France and Belgium to the Royal Newfoundland Regiment which drew its recruits exclusively from that island, then a self-governing Dominion of the British Empire and not a Province of Canada. The Regiment consisted of only one battalion (roughly 1000 men) which could be 'topped up' as necessary with reserves from the island. Of course it was a disaster waiting to happen, as would be discovered on July 1, 1916. Like the equivalent Pals' Battalions from the Midlands and North of England fighting close by, the Newfoundlanders were cut to ribbons. The benefits of battalions made up of relatives, friends and workmates seem at first glance to be obvious but they also posed a huge risk, especially to relatively small or concentrated localised populations. Of the 801 young Newfoundlanders who advanced on July 1 over what is now the Park, only 68 came back.

Today it is a quiet, pastoral haven where sheep may safely graze, and they do a good job too keeping down the grass. Until 2001 there were no facilities at all for visitors except for a toilet in the groundsman's shed, if you knew where to look, that is. In welcome contrast, there's now a large but not obtrusive log-built visitor centre which is staffed by Canadian students.

The Newfoundland Caribou

Like their contemporaries at Vimy Ridge, these young people are unfailingly pleasant and helpful. They come over to France for a year of their university course, working just for their keep and a living allowance. However I would think that the friendships forged on their foreign adventures and the memories of their time on land bought for them by the blood of their countrymen will remain with them for the rest of their lives.

A short distance from the visitor centre is the magnificent Caribou Memorial, one of five erected at the places where the Regiment was most deeply involved during the Great War.

Standing on the mound beside the massive bronze beast, you see before you the area over which the Newfoundlanders attacked. The Park is perhaps the best surviving example of a WWI battlefield still in existence and even more important, one which can be easily comprehended by expert and novice alike. It is also a most "honest" survivor, as all that was done here after 1918 was to dispose of the dangerous bits of detritus left after the fighting. Vestiges remain, an iron picket here, some barbed wire there, but generally, over the years, the grass has merely softened the outlines of the trenches and shell holes and that's it. Come with me on a basic tour.

Probably the best way to tackle the battlefield walk is in a clockwise direction from the Caribou. First is the Danger Tree, a dried old stick of hawthorn now cemented into the ground so frail and dead it is. Reputedly (there's a lot of "reputedlys" and "arguablys" in life, have you noticed?) this is the only thing still standing that was there on "the day".

If memory doesn't fail me, I'm pretty sure it was known as the Tree of Death when I first came here in the early 1980s, so called because many of the men from Newfoundland gathered there when their advance stalled. Unfortunately the line of trees, of which the Death/Danger Tree is the lone survivor, provided the German artillery with a perfect marker with inevitably tragic results for anyone in the vicinity. Now it stands, not defiantly, just a bit forlorn and probably weary, having had to support the burden of history ever since.

A walk in this particular park is especially pleasant on a sunny day in summer when the grass is dry, the sheep are drowsy in the shade of the trees that have grown since the battle and the breeze whispers. How it whispers. Of men who were here and are lost forever. But they're not forgotten, at least not those who are buried in the three cemeteries within the Park boundaries. One of these, Hunter's, while not unique is certainly unusual, being circular in the shape of the shell crater it originally was. Now it's home to 46 men of the Black Watch, which brings me to a significant point. Though this is a memorial park dedicated to the Royal Newfoundland Regiment, and rightly so, it should not be forgotten that it was over this same ground that the men of other regiments also fought and died.

Hunter's Cemetery

51st Highland Division Memorial, Newfoundland Park

As if to emphasise this shared sacrifice, close by the striking figure of a kilted Scotsman gazes out over Y-Ravine. A memorial plaque on the base states, in Gaelic, that it's good to have friends on the day of battle. The lads lying round about would certainly testify to that.

Y-Ravine is a deep mini-glen at the "back" of the Park directly opposite the Caribou, in the shape of a "Y". Maybe you guessed. It's forbidden territory nowadays. I don't know why. It wasn't so in the past when I went down into it on several occasions. The current prohibition is probably to prevent wear and tear or a lawsuit if you slip. Anyway if you go over to the far bank and look back towards the kiltie you can see the entrances to the German tunnels. Looking at them, dug deep into the chalk banks on the side nearest to the Allied lines, it's chillingly obvious why the tons of British shells launched against this particular German position had little or no effect.

Tunnels and all things subterranean are objects of fascination and exaggeration and these are no exception. How far into the banks do they stretch? Exactly how 'luxurious' were they? And is it really possible that they link up with those at nearby Beaumont Hamel thus providing a fireproof conduit to the front line? There's a Ph.D in this for someone! But not for me... I'm off back to the Caribou and the main road.

Before leaving the subject of Newfoundland Park, however, I'd like to quote to you at some length from *Before Endeavours Fade*, the first modern (i.e. post-1970), comprehensive guide to the Western Front. It was written by Rose Coombs who worked for the Imperial War Museum and became, by her own efforts and her enthusiasm, a renowned expert on the old battlefields. Most importantly, through her writings and personal example, she laid down the pathways that are trodden today by those tourists/pilgrims (take your pick!) eager to share in the experiences which so inspired her. I think this passage might explain what I mean.

"Even on a fine summer's day, the Park seems to have a definitely foreboding atmosphere and, after a thunderstorm, I have smelt the awful stench of battle in the still, deep trenches. Nowhere else in my travels on the Western Front has the horror of war come nearer to me than here on one very hot evening following a clear day. It was late July and, as I wandered across the shell-torn slopes towards the German lines, the sound of thunder was heard in the distance, getting gradually nearer as might an artillery barrage. The light grew dim and black clouds gathered overhead. Lightning streaked across the sky – a veritable reincarnation of what a barrage must have been like. As the raindrops began to fall, I dived into one of the trenches for cover and tripped and stumbled along until I found better shelter close to the great Caribou Monument which stands guard over the park from a raised mound above a dugout. All the light I had was a tiny torch and this gave little help in avoiding the occasional shell-case or jagged pieces of iron which litter the trenches. After the hot day, the usual smell of rain-soaked grass began to permeate my nostrils... but with a difference... I realised that this was the smell of battle. It was a never-to-be-forgotten experience and one which I have found on return visits when conditions have been similar."

Phew, missus! Personally, I don't believe a word of it, but it's a good old story and the nearest you're going to get to the supernatural in this particular book. Curious fact – as a complete non-believer but, at the same time, an interested observer, I have never come across any "real" ghost stories or ghostly happenings pertaining to the Great War – and this despite questioning practically every CWGC gardener and barman from Amiens to Ypres. Perhaps before I eventually hand in my final scorecard I may be privy to some spectral fun but I doubt it. Enough of these ravings, it's time to turn right at the Park entrance and wander down to Beaumont-Hamel via Auchonvillers.

En route I pass a common enough sight round here, but one that you certainly don't see back home. On the side of the road next to the entrance of a field is a small pile of shells waiting for the bomb disposal squad. It's hard to get your head round the fact that the Great War has still not finished dealing out death and destruction. Every ploughing time the Grim Reaper goes about his own business, cutting down unfortunate farmers or foolhardy collectors during the perennial Iron Harvest. Making a mental note to mind where I step, I scuttle off down the road to the safety of Auchonvillers or "Ocean Villas" as it was known to the Tommies. Here, the communal graveyard which, like all cemeteries, is worth a browse, contains a line of CWGC

headstones close by the graves of generations of villagers. Nothing unusual in that except that these are of red sandstone, not the customary white Portland stone. Part of an experiment (failed!) to find a cheaper alternative to the limestone apparently. It was also tried at Martinsart, but nowhere else, leaving these oddities for people like me to puzzle over.

Old Beaumont Road leads out of the village down to (surprise!) New Beaumont Road which, in its turn, takes us to Beaumont-Hamel itself. This is Argyll & Sutherland territory, their claim to it being staked forever on November 13, 1916, when they took the village after a titanic struggle. On our walk towards the commune there's much to see and ponder on both sides of the road – Hawthorn Crater, White City and the massive Celtic Cross Memorial to the 8th Argylls.

The 7th and 8th Argylls, who were in the vanguard when Beaumont-Hamel was overrun, are both of interest to me. The 7th drew many of its recruits from Clackmannanshire in Central Scotland where I live while the 8th, with its home in Dunoon, was the battalion of John Lauder. Remember him from Chapter 4?

The History of the 7th A&SH, published in the 1920s, provides us with a graphic description of "the superhuman difficulties" which the troops had to overcome. The Scots nonetheless launched their attack on "the impregnable fortress of Beaumont-Hamel, with its almost ridiculous depth of intricate wire entanglements, its fabulously deep cellars and caves and its picked garrison of the best of the enemy's troops" until, after twelve hours of the bitterest fighting, "it fell at the onslaught of the Jocks". With the village in their hands, these 'Jocks' began to look around and what they found still provides much food for thought.

As might be expected of such enthusiastic fortifiers as the Germans, there was much to discover underground. Nigel Cave, using the Regimental History of the 6th Gordons as a

 source, reveals the relatively luxurious conditions enjoyed by the defenders. In one of the extended cellars there was room for 300 men to shelter "snug and secure". The HQ staff enjoyed the comfort of a floored and panelled living room and there was a kitchen, stoves for heating, electric light and even a four-poster

bed. This last item might well have seen a bit of action but not of a warlike nature, since among items found were articles of lingerie and a lady's slipper. One can only hope that the cat o' nine tails also included in the inventory was solely for military use.

Colonel David Rorie, in his wonderful *A Medico's Luck in the War*, published in the 1920s, describes one particular dugout as "typical of the many with which Beaumont-Hamel was honeycombed... forty steps down to a floored and timbered chamber some 50 feet long, connected to a similar chamber , with a double layer of bunks..."

According to this evidence, the defenders, compared to their attackers, would seem to have been living the proverbial life of Reilly – until their defences crumbled, that is. Rorie stumbled across a particular piece of hell on earth in a chamber full of wounded Germans for whom he could do nothing as they were all suffering from gas-gangrene. Some had already succumbed and he noticed that their "stark" corpses were being greedily gnawed by the omnipresent super-rats. For these men, the good times, if they'd ever had any, were definitely over and now it was their turn to pay the ferryman.

Back to the sunshine and somnolence of Beaumont-Hamel in the afternoon. Things are pretty quiet. They usually are down here, at least in my experience. Amiens is lively, but the villages? Maybe the inhabitants let their hair down in the evening or at weekends but, there again, maybe they don't. Are they all early bedders? Wonder what the birth rate's like? None of my business. Time to return to Thiepval and the car and so it's out of Beaumont-Hamel to Beaucourt, past the station (now a café), and the Ancre British Cemetery wherein lie many of the matelots of the RND, killed on that fateful November day. Perhaps if Edwin had pushed himself just a little bit further he would be lying here now with his comrades in a "hero's" grave, not up there on the Channel coast. No matter. He'd be just as dead.

Now I'm back on the road I came down. Over the Ancre once again, past Ulster Tower and Bob's Yer Uncle! Thiepval's still standing, the car's still in one piece and there's a refreshing shower and a couple of ice cold "*Seize Cents Soixante-Quatres*" waiting for me in Amiens.

Lest you think me overly flippant, dear reader; I'm still haunted by Dyett's fate – and that of all those other lost souls of the Somme.

CHAPTER 7

TOMMY ARMOUR, THE IRON MASTER

THE hardy linksland grass trembles in the keen easterly wind blustering in off the grey North Sea. The hundreds of spectators, mostly men, huddle into their raincoats and clamp their caps ever more firmly on their heads as they trudge through the damp rough. The smoke from their cigarettes and pipes is whipped away towards the town and, with it, flies many a drouthy thought of a warming dram or even a hot pie and a cup of tea. Light rain blows through the air threatening heavier stuff to come. It's mid-afternoon, Friday, June 5, 1931, summertime in Carnoustie.

On the 18th fairway, a tall golfer, easily identified by his trademark black hair, sizes up his shot to the green. After a long period during which he assesses the situation, he sets himself to play. His powerful hands deliver the strike precisely and his approach shot soars towards the pin. Tommy Armour is on the verge of winning golf's greatest prize, the Open Championship.

It had been a long, hard journey back to the east coast of Scotland through the battlefields of France, the rough and

tumble of the burgeoning American golf tour, marital problems and the Wall Street Crash. But he's here at last, after a long self-imposed exile from the land of his youth, ready to win the prize which, above all others, he lusted after. Yes, it had been a lengthy and often arduous odyssey, but, by God, it had been worth it. The chance to join the chosen ones in golf's Valhalla is offered to only a very select few. Tommy Armour, through grit, determination and an unwavering faith in his own ability, was about to book his place at the banqueting table. But how had this lad of relatively humble origins from Edinburgh arrived at his date with destiny on the windswept links of Angus? Let's set sail with him on the voyage of his lifetime and see if we can find out.

Before we cast off, however, may I offer a few words of caution. The details of Tommy Armour's golfing exploits are explicit enough. Just look up the record books. It's some of the other facets of his life that are problematical, to say the least. Perhaps most frustrating is the fact that for a golfer of Armour's undoubted renown no biography exists. Even more surprising is that, given Armour's erudition, no autobiography was penned. Though the two books bearing his name as author are undoubtedly classics of golf instruction, they reveal only tantalising glimpses of the man behind them. Websites and articles dedicated to him there are aplenty but they are, unfortunately, riddled with inaccuracies which frustrate those who go in search of the "real" Silver Scot as he became known as his hair colour changed with age. At the end of this narrative, therefore, I'm going to try to separate the myths from the realities in the hope that some kind of clarity can be achieved. Bearing this caveat in mind, let us now return to the story of a man whose achievements and travails deserve to be remembered.

To begin then at the beginning. Thomas Dickson Armour was born to George and Martha Armour of 18 Balcarres Street, Edinburgh, on the 24th of September, 1896. George Armour was employed at Craighouse Hospital in the Morningside district of Edinburgh as a baker, a good steady

job which would place the family at the top end of the working class. Craighouse, the main treatment centre for the mentally ill in Edinburgh, was opened in 1894 and resembled a typical Victorian country house far removed from the grim asylums for the insane of earlier years.

Operating under a very forward looking regime and with the most modern facilities, it must have provided a pleasant environment for staff and patients alike. George could count himself fortunate indeed to be part of the Craighouse establishment. Unfortunately his good fortune was not to last. In 1900 he succumbed to TB when Tommy was only four. George left Martha, at age 41, as head of the family of six children, three boys and three girls, ranging in age from Sandy at twenty on the topmost perch to Tommy on the bottom rung. Despite this tragic loss, Tommy seems to have had a happy childhood enhanced, as we shall see, by an early introduction to the game of golf.

He received a first class education at the prestigious George Heriot's School situated reasonably close to where he lived, and the benefits of this early exposure to learning remained with Tommy throughout his life. It provided him with the basic tools which enabled him to converse on equal terms with all ranks of society from the crown princes and captains of industry who would come to him in search of the golfing secret right down to the impecunious caddies he met on the links. While a pupil at Heriot's, Tommy was also a member of the Officers' Training Corps (OTC), which partly explains his rapid promotion from humble Private to Second Lieutenant once he was in the "real" army.

At the same time as his mind was being stretched in the classroom and his body on the playing field and parade ground, Tommy was also laying the foundations of his golfing career. From early boyhood he was interested in the game, inspired by the example of his older brothers Sandy and Willie, both of whom would become professionals. Tommy played most of his early golf over the Braid Hills courses near to his home. "The Braids" are municipal courses open to all-comers but, to play in competitions, players have to belong to an affiliated club. Tommy followed in his brothers' footsteps by playing under the banner of the Edinburgh Western Club.

As there were then no tournaments specifically for boys, Tommy was allowed to compete against the men, forcing his way into the Club team at a very young age through a combination of raw talent and dogged determination. There, partnered by Sandy, he helped the Club to success in the very prestigious Dispatch Trophy on at least two occasions, acquiring along the way something of a reputation. According to Frank Moran, the doyen of Scottish golf writers, Armour was "a remarkably confident, even cocky youngster", an attitude that, significantly, "he would retain throughout his life". Thus by natural ability, intense application and the aforementioned "cockiness", young Armour had succeeded by 1914 in thrusting himself into the leading rank of amateur golfers in the Edinburgh area.

But man, or boy, cannot live by clubs alone. What else had the young Armour been up to in those supposedly halcyon years before the Great War? Certainly he had not been neglecting his intellectual development, remaining at Heriot's until 1913 when he left to become a trainee Income Tax Assessor in the Edinburgh branch of the Inland Revenue in Hanover Street. Tommy was now, for a while, caught in the web of the Civil Service, a comfortable trap from which he would be rescued, ironically, by the outbreak of war. Making the best of what was, actually, a pretty good job, Tommy continued his education part-time at Skerry's College, a secretarial establishment which trained young men and women in all aspects of commerce. Situated a stone's throw away from the University of Edinburgh, Skerry's was as close as Tommy was going to get to varsity life .

All in all, the world for Tommy Armour must have been looking mighty fine at the beginning of the 1914 golf season. Unfortunately for him and for thousands of other young men, the golden days were about to vanish in a haze of gunsmoke.

Though Tommy didn't join the Army until late 1915, fifteen months after the outbreak of war, this apparent recalcitrance should not be taken as evidence of any reluctance on his part to serve King and Country. In the first place, he hadn't turned 18 until September, 1914, which was when he would initially have registered for service in the Army, joining the thousands of others who were swamping the recruiting offices. Due to this overwhelming surge of volunteers, it had taken the Army a considerable time to clear the massive backlog in its training programme. Finally, though, Tommy's number came up and, on December 11, 1915, he enrolled in the 5th Battalion of the Royal Scots, the most senior infantry regiment in the British Army. For Private 159696 Armour, T.D., a whole new chapter was about to begin.

At Edinburgh Castle, Tommy "attested" for the "Duration of the War" and then underwent his physical. According to his Medical Inspection Report, he was just under six feet in height, tall for those days, and weighed in at 147 pounds. His chest measurement was a creditable 39 inches with an expansion of 4 inches showing very good lung function. His eyesight, which would later give him great cause for anxiety, was absolutely 100% at this juncture. Overall, his physical development was declared "Good" and he was deemed to be "Fit for Service". Tommy's mother was nominated as his next of kin, his religion was declared to be Presbyterian and his address was given as 23 Comiston Road, a brownstone tenement to which Martha had moved her family after the death of her husband. The paperwork complete, Tommy was now a soldier.

Probably because of his previous experience with Heriot's OTC, Tommy adapted well to the military life, being promoted to the rank of Corporal by April, 1916. He would remain with the Royal Scots on home duty until November, 1916, when he applied for promotion to officer rank and was transferred to the Machine Gun Corps as a Second Lieutenant. Army life certainly seems to have agreed with Tommy, if the findings of his pre-promotion medical are anything to go by. By the time he joined the Machine Gun Officer Cadet Battalion at Bisley, he had put on 28 pounds and now presented a much more imposing figure than the slim lad who had joined the colours in 1915.

While Tommy was following the path to promotion in Britain, strange shapes roared out of the mist towards the German lines one September morning on the Somme. The tanks had arrived. Although initially achieving only very limited success, the potential of these 'iron-clad monsters' did not go unnoticed by the generals and, as more machines rolled off the assembly lines in England, crews were sought to man them. Consequently, an offshoot of the Machine Gun Corps, the Heavy Branch, was formed at the end of 1916 to fill this manpower shortage. As Second Lieutenant Armour had been showing considerable prowess both in handling machine guns and in instructing their gunners, he was an obvious choice to join this new section which was rebadged on 28 July, 1917, as the Tank Corps.

The Machine Gun Corps, Heavy Branch

Unfortunately, little is known of Tommy's career in the Tank Corps. We know the date he arrived in France and when he was incapacitated and that's about it. We may reasonably assume that he experienced the same discomforts and dangers endured by all "tankies". The working conditions were appalling. Petrol fumes choked the crewmen, the constant noise of the engine and guns deafened them and the concentration of enemy fire often made them sitting ducks. Nevertheless the "metal monsters" played a significant role in the eventual Allied victory, and Tommy Armour was undoubtedly part of it.

Arriving in France in March, 1918, Tommy avoided misfortune until his luck ran out in May of the same year when he sustained severe mustard gas damage to his eyes. Hospitalised at Le Treport on the Channel Coast, Tommy remained in France until 5 August, 1918, when he sailed for Dover aboard a hospital ship. Back on home soil once more, he was sent to the 3rd London General Hospital in Wandsworth where he remained for almost three months undergoing treatment for "severe corneal opacity following ulceration". Both eyes had been severely damaged, particularly his left in which he would effectively be blind for the rest of his life. Discharged from Wandsworth in late October, 1918, Tommy returned to Edinburgh to convalesce at home. Unfortunately his eyes were still giving him huge cause for concern, as the document "Proceedings of a Medical Board" reveals. Far from having recovered his sight in any satisfactory way, he was still suffering from "severe micropurulent conjunctivitis complicated by corneal ulceration of the left eye" which had resulted in a "nebula" covering "the papillary area of the cornea". Adding to Tommy's visual problems was the complication that the damage to his right eye, though of a lesser nature than that affecting his left, was nonetheless still troubling him.

But what does all this mean in practical terms? Let plain Tommy Armour, no longer a Second Lieutenant, having been medically discharged from the Army on November 30, 1918, tell us himself. On December 7, 1918, he wrote, in what might be described as an educated fist, the following letter from his home in Edinburgh to the War Office in London in support of his claim for a disability pension.

Sir,
I had the honour to receive your letter of 30th ult [sic], telling me that my last medical board had passed me unfit and that I was to relinquish my commission on account of ill health.

Quoting your statement, "under the circumstances of the medical board passing you still unfit for further service and that you have had all the sick leave to which you are entitled, there is no alternative but to Gazette you as relinquishing your commission on account of ill health."

The circumstances under which I left the 3rd London General Hospital were that I was given one month's special leave under A.C.1, 905, PARA IV and I was to return to hospital for further treatment which my eye still needs.

Quoting your letter again, "The case will be submitted to the Ministry of Pensions for their consideration as to any claim to retired pay or gratuity on account of disability".

Surely there is something wrong there. The condition I am in just now is this and I have medical proof. My left eye is useless for good. I am not absolutely blind in it but, to put it another way, without my right eye I would be of no use. That is my left one. My right eye is very weak and I have to wear blue glasses every day.

Surely, sir, I am entitled to a pension under these conditions? I would like to go through a pensions board in London after some more treatment, so could I have a warrant to travel to London?

Hoping to have your consideration.
I have the honour to be, Sir,
Your obedient servant,
Thomas D. Armour (2nd Lieutenant)

Good old War Office! That's the way to go! Stuff malingerers like Tommy and the million or so others who were trying to scrounge disability pensions! Weren't there plenty of street corners to sell bootlaces and matches on? What more could these men want? By Jove, some of the blighters have even been given artificial legs and arms...

Now we know why Second Lieutenant Thomas D. Armour, dismissed from the service to save money on his wages, decided to switch allegiance from his 'grateful' country to the Land of Opportunity as soon as he was able. To be fair, we don't know whether or not Tommy got the financial help that he and the thousands like him so richly deserved. We don't even know if he got the three medals to which he was entitled – the British War Medal, the Victory Medal and the Silver War Badge.

Whatever, it's reasonable to suppose that, in early 1919, thoughts of ever playing golf again at all, never mind at championship standard, would have been pretty far from the 22 year old's mind. For this particular Tommy, the Great War was most definitely over. Fortunately it would not be too long before he could sally forth once more. This time, however, the battleground would be one of his own choosing and the only dangerous missile an occasional misdirected golf ball.

Now we come to the easy bit in Tommy's story, his postwar golfing career. It's all there in the record books. With that in mind, I'll take you on a tour of the highlights and try to show you how Tommy's wartime experiences gave him a decidedly different perspective on the challenge of championship golf. Though he wouldn't be laying his life on the line this time, his skill, nerve and, most important, his pride would all to be put to the test.

As the poppies bloomed on the now peaceful fields of Flanders, so did the urge to play golf blossom in the soul of Tommy Armour. His left eye was still, and would remain, a mere passenger for the rest of his life, but the sight had been fully restored to his right, which meant that, with a few adjustments as to how he lined up his shots, Tommy was set to go once more. The blue glasses were discarded forever and the green grass lay before him. It was late spring, 1919.

Tommy found his game was still intact. All it required was competition to hone it to its old sharpness and maybe beyond. Playing in Edinburgh at the Braids and out at Lothianburn, Tommy was soon back in the winning groove and, heartened by this local success, he decided to take his game further afield. During that first postwar summer, he managed to place well in good amateur tournaments – most notably as runner-up in the Highland Open at Pitlochry and second medallist in the inaugural Eden Tournament at St Andrews.

It should be pointed out that these results were achieved with a putter that proved so fickle that it was hurled to a watery grave from an Edinburgh bound train while crossing the Forth Bridge. His solution to his putting woes was simply to improve his iron play so that he stuck his shots to the green closer to the hole. As a result he transformed himself from an excellent iron player into a superb one, becoming a great 'clutch' putter in the process.

Tommy's military experiences may have given him some perspective on his shortcomings with the putter. As he revealed later in his book, *How to Play Your Best Golf All the Time*:

> "...I've been in some tight spots apart from golf where the danger and the possible loss were infinitely greater than any that can be associated with putting... Yet I've had more difficulty in controlling my nervous reactions in putting... especially in championship competition. How can I explain that? I can't."

Rather wryly he observed that "Love and putting are mysteries for the philosopher to solve". Given his experiences in both of these fields of play, he might well have been right.

Reasonably satisfied with his return to competitive play, Tommy set his goals much higher for the next season.

1920 saw his star really begin to ascend as winner of the prestigious French Amateur Championship, a victory which Frank Moran regarded as "no surprise". On the back of this success, Tommy set sail in early July on an exploratory trip to America to see what goodies might be on offer in Uncle Sam's fair land.

Lady Luck, who had accompanied him through most of the War, did not desert him now. On the voyage to the States he was befriended by none other than the legendary (and I do mean 'legendary') American professional, Walter Hagen, who was returning from his disastrous debut in the Open Championship a wiser but, typically, not a sadder man.

Obviously the flamboyant "Haig" could see in his young protégé a potential kindred spirit, one who might also take time off along life's highway "to smell the flowers". Be that as it may, Hagen came through for his new pal in a big way. Using the considerable clout enjoyed by those golfers who have won a Major, "Sir Walter", twice American Open Champion, persuaded the prestigious Westchester-Biltmore Golf Club in New York State to take on the amateur Armour as their secretary at a reputed salary of $10,000 per annum, an astronomical sum for the time. Tommy, as we shall see, was going to be very grateful indeed for this incredible stroke of good fortune.

At this point it might be appropriate to reemphasise that much of the Armour story is shrouded in myth and mystery, some of his own creation I guess, but the rest merely the result of it being nobody's business but his own. Who, for example, sponsored him to the extent that he could travel, not only to France, but also to America, to play golf? I doubt if that war pension he'd been forced to beg the War Office for would have taken him much further than a tram ride along Princes' Street in his hometown. In contrast, what he was about to receive at Westchester would have enabled him to buy the tram and still have some pocket money left over. Tommy's mystery benefactor in Edinburgh had thrown him a lifeline which allowed him to survive financially while returning to golf. Hagen's recommendation meant that Tommy would now be able to further his golfing career in the States under his own steam. The man from Morningside was not about to let such a golden opportunity slip away.

In taking the plunge Stateside, Armour was merely treading a pathway already well worn by the brogues of the many golfers who had left the east coast of Scotland, especially Carnoustie, to ply their trade in America. Their grip on American golf became more of a stranglehold, at least until 1911 when the first American, the ultimately tragic Johnny McDermott, finally broke through to win his nation's national championship. A repeat performance by McDermott the next year followed by young Francis Ouimet's astounding upset of the two great English pros, Vardon and Ray, in 1913 meant that golf was firmly established in American minds as a "proper" sport worthy of the attention of all red-blooded fans.

By the time Tommy stepped off the liner in New York in the late summer of 1920, golf was booming and the Twenties were just about to start roaring. Undoubtedly he was in the right place at exactly the right time. And, given his tenacity and personality, both of which had been tested and tempered in the fires of the Great War, it should not surprise us that Tommy did rather well. Starting with runner-up spot in the 1920 Canadian Open, Tommy went on to compile a very useful amateur record before turning pro in 1924. Though the decision to leave the comfort zone of Westchester-Biltmore must have been a difficult one, Tommy realised that, if he was going to reach the pinnacle of golfing fame, he could afford no outside distractions, no matter how well paid these were.

During this period before he went pro, Tommy seems to have returned to his native heath very seldom. His only reported visit to Edinburgh occurred in January, 1921, when he appeared back in Edinburgh accompanied by a "ribbed wedge" and, surprisingly – *very* surprisingly for one person in particular – a Spanish wife. Tommy's new wedge excited much interest as the latest 'thing' from the USA. The wife, of whom we shall later hear much more, created a similar buzz, the reverberations from which would pursue Tommy down the rest of the decade.

It is not my intention to write a history of the golf scene in the 1920s and 30s. It's enough to point out that, by the mid-twenties, the centre of the golfing universe had shifted from Britain to the USA. Indeed, the years from 1925 to the early thirties in America might quite reasonably be dubbed "Golf's First Golden Age", a period with more than its fair share of stellar personalities, not the least of whom was Tommy Armour.

Briefly, his record reads as follows. Among his many other victories, Armour, by then a naturalised American, had won two Majors, the U.S. Open in 1927 and the PGA championship in 1930. He had also won the Western Open in 1929, a tournament that, in the absence of the Masters which didn't begin until 1934, was regarded by the Americans as a Major. So, if Armour could bag a British Open he'd have the full set and would join the select few at the very top of the golfing tree. Which brings us back to where our story began.

Once again, it's afternoon in Carnoustie on Friday, June 5, 1931, and Tommy Armour is on the final 18 holes in the Open Championship. His previous three rounds had been mediocre to say the least, especially the 77 he'd carded that morning. The only things in his favour were that the other challengers were also struggling while he himself was "playing badly well". In truth he might have been in a much worse position as he embarked on his final round. Five shots back was a significant deficit, but not an insurmountable one. If ever he needed to find his game, this was the time. And find it he most certainly did.

As *Golf Illustrated* reported at the time, "...stout-hearted Tommy Armour came into his own and won as brave a victory as has been ever recorded in the history of the Open Championship..."

Much like his fellow Scot, Paul Lawrie, would do 68 years later over the same course, Tommy came through the field with a magnificent last round to claim the title he wanted above all others. His friend and fellow competitor, Henry Cotton, the great English player, was moved to write in that same golfing journal, "Of pluck he is just chock-full. There is never a score that he feels he cannot attain...

Tommy is not the fellow to give up. He will fight and keep fighting with unbounded grit and determination".

Bravery, pluck, grit. These are not words to be used lightly. However, bravery does have a part to play in all forms of sporting endeavour. Not the bravery of the battlefield admittedly, but an ability to hold one's nerve when all around are losing their's. Macdonald Smith, the aforequoted Cotton and, most notably, the almost tragic Jose Jurado, all let the claret jug slip from their grasp on that final round, victims of their own inner demons. For Cotton, his time would come later over this same track in 1937. For the others their chance had gone forever. Tommy had won the tournament that he later revealed to Frank Moran "...was the hardest to win for my heart was really set on it". Not to mention the difficulty of playing in Scotland in front of fellow Scots as an American citizen.

Perhaps it's worth considering the fact that, of the four leading contenders for the crown, only Armour had endured the dangers of the battlefield. If it didn't break a man, as it did many poor souls, the experience gained on the muddy fields of Flanders might well have been of immense help in any future crisis. Described by the *Glasgow Herald* correspondent as "an all-steel man", Tommy, I suspect, could draw on memories far removed from the golf course to help him hit the vital shots while under the most intense pressure. His final round of 71 was celebrated by the same scribe as "a triumph of nerve and staying power". The greatest "closer out" the game has ever known, certainly up to the time of Jack Nicklaus, had closed out just when he needed it most.

Tommy's victory at Carnoustie marked the *apogée* of his competitive career. There would be other successes, most notably in the Canadian Open in 1934, but essentially he began to wind down as the 1930s rolled on. Ironically, his ball striking, especially with the irons, remained majestic. It was the weakness on the greens alluded to earlier that came back to haunt him – in spades. He fell victim to "the yips", a term coined by Armour himself to describe the nervous twitching of the putter, which meant that even the easiest of putts became a nightmare. Up to the green, he was still "the Iron Master", but once on the dance floor he was done. This time there would be no solution; the yips were there to stay. As he himself reflected later, "Once you've had 'em, you've got 'em". So, ever the realist, he gave up regular competitive play.

However, someone of Tommy's acute intelligence and ability was not likely to disappear from the golfing scene in a hurry. Instead he made himself into the first golfing guru and in the process made a second fortune far outstripping the one he'd lost in the aftermath of the 1929 Wall Street Crash and a costly divorce. Captains of industry and stars of the silver screen and the sports arena flocked to the practice ground at Boca Raton in Florida. There they ingested Tommy's pearls of golfing wisdom which he dispensed from under a large multi-coloured sun umbrella. For a fee, of course. And what fees they were. All the days of struggle from a fatherless boyhood in Edinburgh, through war-torn France to the cut and thrust of the American Tournament circuit and the white heat of the Majors, at last made financial sense in the shade at Boca Raton. But there was more to come.

Tommy produced the blockbuster of all golf instructional books, *How to Play Your Best Golf All the Time*, in 1953. Though ghosted by Herb Graffis, Tommy's input was huge. In fact, Tommy, an articulate and literate man, was quite capable of writing such a book under his own steam and rumour has it that he was doing Herb a favour for his support in the past. It's worth noting that the best-selling sequel, *A Round of Golf with Tommy Armour*, seems to have been written by the man himself.

Cashing in further on his reputation, Tommy also endorsed a signature line of golf clubs which proved to be so successful that they're still being manufactured today.

Well cushioned by the fortune he had amassed from his teaching, books, equipment manufacture and very sound investments, Tommy lived out his final years in almost regal splendour as pro emeritus at Winged Foot Golf Club, New York, with big brother Sandy as his next-door neighbour.

Tommy Armour died in 1968, aged 72. His posthumous election to the Golf Hall of Fame in 1976 simply confirmed what all interested parties already knew – that Tommy, the Black Scot who became the Silver Scot, was one of golf's all-time greats.

So we might end our story, a rather bland picture of a golfing legend. And that's probably how Tommy would have wanted it. But there's much more to the Armour story than what you've just read. For instance, to what was I referring when I hinted at problems caused by what turned out to be his first marriage? I suppose that it's none of my business to probe, tabloid style, into someone's personal affairs – especially when that 'someone' is in no position to respond. However, information on Tommy's private life uncovered purely by chance in the course of my research means that an inquisitive being like myself cannot help going down the investigative road just to see what's at the end. And thereby hangs yet another tale – or several tales.

Tommy's first marriage, for instance, reveals an episode in his life which, though mildly amusing to the dispassionate observer, must have been embarrassing, painful even, to those involved. After he joined the Royal Scots in December, 1915, Tommy remained in Edinburgh for the best part of a year, during which time a mutual interest in the violin led to him meeting a young lady, Marie Catherine Young. He continued to see Miss Young on his return from the War when he, allegedly, had promised her a little more than just to keep practising on the fiddle.

I first came across Marie in an article entitled "Noted Golfer Sued" in *The Scotsman*, dated May, 1929. She was attempting to grab Tommy's share of the proceeds of a challenge match which had been played at Dalmahoy Golf Club on the outskirts of Edinburgh. The players involved were Tommy and his stalwart pal and fellow expat, "Wee Bobby" Cruickshank, against the Englishmen, Charles Whitcombe and the up and coming Henry Cotton. Miss Young was claiming £300 plus court expenses and interest of £120 in payment of an award made in her favour in 1921 for breach of promise. Eight years later, here was Marie still hot on the trail of her one-time man. To paraphrase Congreve, "Hell hath no fury like a woman scorned – especially if she's blessed with a long memory". The 1929 arrestment failed, but what was behind it all?

With a little help from my relatives in the legal profession, all can be revealed. In February, 1921, at the Court of Session in Edinburgh, William McWhirter, the editor of *The Weekly Record*, a Glasgow scandal sheet, was in the dock charged with Contempt of Court having rehashed some articles from the English rags. This information pertaining to Marie's suit against our Thomas was "*sub judice*" in Scotland at the time and should not have been published. Fortunately, for seekers of wisdom and truth like myself, the February 5, 1921, edition of *The Weekly Record* has survived, dusty and dog-eared, but still very accessible, in the Mitchell Library, Glasgow. So let's have a look at the offending article.

LOVE ON THE GOLF LINKS

CHAMPION "HAUNTED BY SPANISH GIRL"

SHE FASCINATED ME!

"It was a great mistake, but she fascinated me beyond everything. I could not help it. She fascinated me on golf courses until I did not know what I was doing, and then we got married."

Such is an extract from a letter which was read in the Edinburgh Court of Session during the hearing of an action brought by Miss Marie Catherine Young, a violinist of Iona Street, Leith, against Thomas Dickson Armour of Comiston Road, Edinburgh, for £2000 for breach of promise of marriage.

Mr Armour is the amateur golf champion of France and has just completed a long tour in America.

According to the pursuer, he and Miss Young met in December, 1916, and in the spring of 1917 they became engaged to be married, Miss Young then being 22 years old.

Their marriage was delayed through various circumstances... Mr Armour was for a time in the Army and also had many golfing engagements, one of which kept him in America for several months.

Before he started for America it was arranged that the marriage was to take place as soon as possible after his return.

He wrote to her that he was looking forward to the happy times they were to have and concluded: "I do hope they won't be long in coming".

On another occasion he wrote: "I will be able to have you all to myself forever".

MARRIED A SPANIARD!

On December 16, 1920, Miss Young received from Mr Armour the following letter:

November 16, 1920.

My Dear Marie,

Probably by this time you will have heard all about it. Well, I have made the greatest mistake I ever made in all my life and already I have realised it.

I was married two weeks ago in New York to a Spanish girl.

Now, Marie, I know what you must say about me and, believe me, everything you say has already been fulfilled.

Oh dear, when I think and sit alone as I am just now, I can realise what I have done, but at the time I did not. I could not write to you before as I could not get her out of my mind and, naturally, I did not feel like writing.

I hope you will forgive me, Marie, as I have already had my punishment. I am coming home myself, I think.

Please do not mention a word of this to a single soul, I mean about my predicament.

Yours, with regret,

Tommy

Mr Armour, in his defence, denies that he ever promised to marry the violinist and, in any case, contends the damages claimed are excessive.

As we already know, Tommy, far from "coming home myself", brought his new bride, the former Miss Consuelo Cordoba, back to Edinburgh, along with his ribbed wedge. Alerted to her ex-beloved's presence on home turf, Marie promptly hit him with the breach of promise suit for £2000 which resulted in victory for her but with a much reduced financial award of £300 and costs. Unfortunately her success ensured that Tommy and his Spanish fireball vamoosed back to the States with some alacrity leaving the bill unpaid. It also might explain why Tommy played only twice (1926 and 1929) in the Open before his 1931 expedition to Carnoustie. Given the 1929 clawback attempt by Marie, you can sort of grasp his logic. I've really no idea how often he returned 'home' during the twenties but I'm guessing his visits were few. Up until 1924 he was employed at Westchester and then he was on the circuit so, with the time it took to make the transatlantic crossing in those days, there would have been little opportunity for visiting friends and family back in Edinburgh. Especially with Marie and her lawyer hovering in the wings.

Tommy certainly seems to have paid for his "mistake" in a big way. His union with the Spanish Rose produced one child, Tommy Jr., and, eventually, a "highly publicised" and expensive divorce. I suspect that Consuelo was of a suspicious nature if the following from Norman Mair's excellent article in *The Scotsman* of December 27, 1977, is anything to go by:

> "When Henry Cotton went to America in 1928-29, Armour took him under his wing, Cotton in return undertaking the infinitely difficult diplomatic task of answering the phone to Armour's wife when she rang their room late in the evening to check that her husband was either safely tucked up in bed or on his way there."

Not much trust there, then. Unsurprisingly the divorce court was just around the corner. Shortly after Consuelo and Tommy parted company in 1930, he married Estelle Andrews, reportedly a woman of infinite good humour, and they lived, so far as this outsider can guess, happily ever after.

Sadly I don't know anything further about Marie. Hopefully she wouldn't assume the role of Leith's answer to Miss Havisham with no great expectations, condemned to a life of tea and sympathy and "Fascination" on the fiddle. Someone to help her forget and give her a good time would have been nice. Consuelo sounds like she could take very good care of herself.

The only other comment I dare make on the subject of our Tommy and the opposite sex is that some of his friends from Hollywood, notably Mr Errol Flynn, were not renowned for having adopted a monk-like lifestyle. There we shall leave the realm of speculation and rumour and instead take a look at how Tommy was perceived by those who knew him best, both professionally and personally.

On the links, Tommy Armour was the business – ice-cool, deliberate and, given the slightest opportunity, lethal. As he himself put it, "Happily, I am blessed with a temperament that has made me immune to the first tee version of stage fright". But Tommy was much more than a mere golfing machine, able to deliver the goods when the going got tough. Frank Moran, who knew Armour better than most, reveals that, away from the heat of battle, he had "irrepressible gaiety and humour bubbling near the surface and apt to erupt at erratic intervals... dropping hints and wisecracks and dissolving with laughter the image of the Scot as a dour, spiky character".

Tommy worked hard at projecting this alternative image. Indeed, so successful were his efforts that he became, once again according to Moran, "a figure larger even than the outsize life he led. Humorous but authoritative, a showman in the rollicking, swashbuckling sense that Walter Hagen was one".

As part of his "showman" persona, Tommy reputedly could tear a pack of cards in half. Quite a trick. He could also hold a billiard cue by the tip at arm's length. If you think that sounds easy, just try it. The great Jack Dempsey, the Manassas Mauler, Heavyweight Champion of the World from 1919 to 1926, did, and lost the bet to our Tom. However the large hands which enabled Tommy to accomplish such feats could also be used in much gentler pursuits. Those violin sessions with Marie back in Edinburgh had not been wasted and Tommy enjoyed making music for the rest of his life, sometimes playing to entertain his friends but, more often, just for his own pleasure.

Besides this interest in music Tommy was also a devotee of literature. His self-penned *A Round of Golf with Tommy Armour* reveals, for example, considerable familiarity with not only John Bunyan's *The Pilgrim's Progress* but also Coleridge's *The Rime of the Ancient Mariner*. Partly as a result of his reading he tended to be very loquacious with a definite leaning towards using language that showed off not only his erudition but also his keen sense of humour. According to Norman Mair, Tommy was "a compulsive but entertaining talker with the born raconteur's licence to embroider" and, as such, he could be guaranteed to keep his listeners highly entertained. The very fact that he took to the bright, well-educated Henry Cotton, who remained a lifelong friend, indicates the kind of companion Armour most appreciated, someone who could converse with him on subjects far removed from the locker room.

Yet this 'gentler' side to his character sits somewhat at odds with the picture of Armour, the monumental drinker, under his sunshade at Boca Raton with a table, described by

Henry Cotton

143

Herb Graffis as "so crowded with tall glasses that it looked as if at any moment he might launch into a pipe-organ recital". Allegedly, according to the great American golf writer, Herbert Warren Wind, Tommy "liked to punctuate his teaching sessions with liquid nourishment. His standard drink was a concoction called a Gin Buck... a stiff shot of gin diluted by ginger ale and slices of lemon and lime. This was followed by a tall Scotch and Soda... and a Bromo Seltzer... Armour's drinking routine at his lesson tee became legendary and remained so until he died..."

Note the word "legendary". I'll be dealing with this side of the Tommy Armour story in the Afterword to this chapter. Meanwhile let's just say that Tommy must have been almost superhuman merely to survive such a daily alcoholic onslaught on his liver, let alone have a head clear enough to teach his pupils who were paying so much for the privilege. The fact that they continued to clamour for more of his wisdom suggests that Tommy's drinking, like that of his friend, Walter Hagen, might well have been more apparent than real. It's reckoned that, during his golfing career, Hagen tipped away more booze into flower vases than ever went down his throat but he never let his unsuspecting rivals know that. Maybe Tommy was the same.

An extract from his book *A Round of Golf with Tommy Armour* nicely connects Tommy's orotundity (love of flowery language, dear) with his liking for "a wee refreshment". On a hole close to the clubhouse, he proposes to his pupil that they make "a slight detour towards the club's life-saving station for a dipper of internal liniment". One thing's certain; he didn't try to hide his liking for spirituous liquor behind a facade of hypocrisy, and he appears never to have regretted for a minute his love affair with the bottle.

Whether or not he deserved his playboy reputation, I think Tommy might well have revelled in this rather raffish persona and worked hard to present it to his public. On the other hand, I suspect Tommy the Roisterer was largely a façade concealing a more sensitive soul lurking behind it. Much more important, most people who entered Tommy's fiefdom seemed to have liked being there. The only slightly adverse comment I have come across is that made by Charles Price who revealed that, occasionally, Armour could display an acerbic turn of phrase. Perhaps not so surprising when one considers the many hopeless cases, in golfing terms, who came to him hoping for miracles.

There we have him, then – except that, of course, we don't. At this point in time, far removed from the characters and events, trying to capture the essence of Armour is like trying to catch the proverbial lightning in a bottle. So I think it's best to leave the last words on our hero to Norman Mair of *The Scotsman* once again, and to the Silver Scot himself. Read them and enjoy them. First of all, Mair :

> "Tommy Armour was a man who revelled in the limelight and yet never made the mistake of taking himself too seriously. A man who never kept a newspaper cutting or a trophy but kept instead a sense of proportion."

And, finally, Tommy Armour, the Iron Master:

> "It's nice to be a good golfer and win championships but, hell, being the finest

golfer in the world never cured anyone of polio."

* * *

Afterword

I've been interested in Tommy Armour ever since 1953 when I first read *How to Play Your Best Golf All the Time*, yet I've been able to find out relatively little about him. In most of what I've written, I've had to rely on previously published newspaper and magazine articles. My only original research has been through the archive documents pertaining to his birth and his war record, and contemporary newspapers and journals. Consequently I'm left with the distinctly frustrated feeling of being within touching distance of the great man but not quite making the final, vital connection. "*C'est la vie, c'est la guerre*", I suppose, as Tommy himself might well have said!

The information available on Tommy Armour which exists, largely on the Internet, contains many errors, some of which may well have been encouraged by Armour himself. In an attempt to set the record straight, allow me to review the most obvious mistakes and the occasional "mystery". I have already touched on some of these issues in my narrative, but I think that they are worth reiterating.

Birthdate
I've been to Register House in Edinburgh where I've handled Tommy's actual birth certificate and obtained a copy of it. His birth date is, conclusively, September 24, 1896, not 1895, as is so often misreported.

Accommodation

When the family moved after George Armour's death from their flat in Balcarres Street to another apartment in nearby Comiston Road, it's hard to tell whether this was through economic necessity or choice. Judging by my expedition to the properties, the Comiston Road apartment block looks to be a superior address to the one in Balcarres Street, with all due respect to the current residents. It's more than likely that Tommy's five siblings, who were considerably older than him, were bringing in a relatively substantial family income making possible such an upmarket move.

Education

Tommy went to George Heriot's School, not Fettes College – or even "Fettys" as I saw it on one website. He did not attend the University of Edinburgh, let alone graduate from it. He did, however, attend Skerry's College in Edinburgh as part of his Civil Service training.

Army Career

Having obtained the relevant documents from the National Archive in London, I can with confidence state that Tommy's most senior rank was Second Lieutenant, not "Major" as is so often quoted. With regard to his war wounds, the only documentary evidence which survives quite definitely supports the fact of his partial blinding by mustard gas. However there is no indication that he had steel plates in his head and arm. Though this damage could have occurred at the same time as his gassing, there is no mention of it in his records. I've also seen the story that Armour killed a German with his bare hands and suspect this is just a myth. Tommy was in a tank and so it would have been unlikely, though not impossible, that he would have been in man-to-man combat. There's also a belief that he was presented to King George V and received a gallantry award for this deed. This is untrue. Any such medal award would have been 'gazetted'. This means that the announcement of the award and an account of the action would appear in *The London Gazette*. No such evidence exists to support this claim. He may well have had a visit from the King on one of the monarch's frequent visits to the hospitals at Le Treport or Wandsworth but Tommy would just have been one among many getting the royal nod.

With regard to Tommy's medals, he would have been eligible for three, none of which refers to gallant deeds on the battlefield. They are the British War Medal, the Victory Medal and the Silver War Badge, the latter being awarded to those servicemen who were discharged due to sickness or wounds, in Tommy's case the effects of the mustard gas.

None of this contradictory evidence detracts in any way from Tommy's very meritorious war record. He did his duty on the battlefield and his bravery, like that of so many of his contemporaries, is unquestioned.

Golf – and some more romance!

Tommy's golfing achievements are accurately documented and indisputable. The only point I would make is that Sandy Armour, Tommy's eldest brother, was never the Scottish Amateur Champion as has been reported, though he was a golfer of repute in Scotland both prior to and after WWI. The solution to the "mystery" of how Tommy financed his amateur career post-WWI, especially his expeditions to France and the USA in 1920, might lie in the court reports of the 1921 breach of promise case. Here his profession is referred to as "rubber manufacturer". This suggests to me that he had a sinecure post with, probably, the North British Rubber Company of Edinburgh, a firm well-known for the manufacture of golf balls. Tommy's "job" would be to represent the North British Company and to publicise their

products. What better way could he do this than by playing golf? Incidentally, this court report refers to him as "Thomas DONALDSON Armour". How this glaring error occurred and remained uncorrected is yet another mystery. Suffice to say, the defendant erroneously referred to is indeed our man. On the other hand, I've received information via Tommy's grandson, Jock Armour, that the "mystery sponsor" was, in fact, his first wife Consuelo Cortina Carerra de Cajiga who was a very wealthy young woman in her own right. Additionally I've also learned via Jock that Tommy met Consuelo in Britain where she was travelling with a chaperone before he went to the States for the first time.

Conclusion
When all is said and done, one thing remains certain. Tommy Armour was a great golfer, one of the greatest of all time. The half-truths and myths can't detract from that. Do they really matter anyway? After all, as the editor of "The Shinbone Star" says at the end of John Ford's great Western, *The Man*

Who Shot Liberty Valance, "This is the West, sir. When the legend becomes fact, print the legend!"

CHAPTER 8

AN AUTUMN INTERLUDE, SEPTEMBER 2010

S EPTEMBER is, arguably, the best time to visit the battlefields of the Somme and Flanders. There's always the prospect of an Indian Summer, the crowds have thinned out and the crops are gone, exposing the chalky outlines of the trenches and shell-holes in the fields of Picardy and Belgium. So, here we go once more, to retread old paths and to meet old friends, some, happily, still hale and hearty, others dead for almost a century now, but not forgotten.

Travelling south into France from the ferryport at Zeebrugge, motorists on the autoroutes get little or no sense of the battlefields apart from an occasional familiar name on a motorway sign. It's only after leaving the *péage* at Bapaume and taking the road to Albert that the traces of conflict really begin to make their presence felt.

First sighting is the British Cemetery at Warlencourt. There it is, on the left-hand side of the road, just short of the infamous Butte of the same name, the taking of which proved so costly to the Pals from Durham. Through Le Sars and Courcelette with its roadside *friterie* and on to Pozieres, passing all the while increasing numbers of CWGC cemetery signs. Tractors with huge trailers are in action gathering up the harvested potatoes and sugar beet and, no doubt, the detritus of battles past. Inevitably, some of this abandoned ordnance can prove rather tricky, a fact very forcibly brought home to us by this discovery the next day.

Fortunately the driver escaped unscathed but his new John Deere didn't; a bitter blow to his annual profits as there is no insurance cover for such mishaps, so frequently do they occur.

About half a mile through Pozières, the white stones of Ovillers Military Cemetery draw us to our first encounter. Every year I visit the grave of John Lauder, the subject of Chapter 4 of this book. Standing there looking down the slope of Mash Valley towards the village of La Boisselle, it's impossible to imagine the carnage that once occurred hereabouts but it is possible to feel the warmth of the sun and hear the ripe maize whispering in the gentle breeze. Over at 2

o'clock, the Golden Madonna atop the Basilique at Albert hoists her glittering baby to the heavens. And life goes on.

I suppose one of the biggest problems encountered by the not quite so dedicated travelling companion on a battlefield trip is the "Oh, no! Not another bloody graveyard!" syndrome. But that's the price one has to pay, if, indeed, it can be considered to be a price, in order to understand the past. Graveyards, whether on the Somme or just in our own backyard, tell us how we used to live – and die – and perhaps how we've become who we are. The immaculate cemeteries of the Western Front not only give us the chance to remember those who went long before their time was due but they also allow us to see and appreciate the never-ending work of the CWGC.

The Sword of Sacrifice, Ovillers Cemetery

Leaving John and his companions to their endless sleep in Ovillers Cemetery and the subject of the CWGC to a later chapter, we motor on to Amiens and here I shall make a recommendation. If you happen to be in the city between May and September or at Christmas, check out the *son et lumière* at the Cathedral. This takes place every night and is extremely impressive. Not long ago, when contractors were cleaning the stonework of the building, lingering traces of medieval pigment were found on the many small statues festooning the facade. Painted figures like these were apparently the Church's way in the Middle Ages of providing locals and visitors alike with a graphic understanding of the Bible, almost like a comic strip in stone. Nowadays, by the use of lasers, the statues are displayed nightly in their original, breathtaking colours. The gasps of wonder from the audience are testament to their enduring power to amaze and entertain, just one of those little extras that can be tacked on to a battlefield trip. It's always worthwhile visiting local tourist offices to see what non-military delights are on offer. But, of course, the main point of any trip to the Somme is to explore those places where momentous military events once occurred and so the road from Albert to Bapaume beckons once again.

Most of the sites on our must-see list for this trip will be familiar to readers but I make no apologies for revisiting them. Despite its familiarity, the great '*Trou de Mine*' – the huge mine crater – at La Boisselle continues to cast its spell and not far away, at the massive *Memorial to the Missing of the Somme* at Thiepval, the 600 graves in the Anglo-French cemetery to the rear of the monument, bear witness to a common bond of suffering.

Thiepval is the starting point for that walk over the valley of the Ancre to Newfoundland Park and Beaumont

Hamel which was mentioned in a previous chapter. On quiet country roads all the way, it's a fine trek in its own right but the experience will be greatly enhanced if you can appreciate the significance of your surroundings. For this it's probably best to have the guidance of someone familiar with military geography as well as history. In our case we were fortunate enough to have the services of a friend, Alan Marquis from Guernsey, whom we'd arranged to meet at Ulster Tower. With Alan in charge we set off for an afternoon of exploration, first to Newfoundland Park to hear tales of the tunnels of Y-Ravine. As we proceed, Alan's expertise in relating the features of trench maps from WWI to the topography of today clicks in. The location of the Sunken Road near Beaumont-Hamel is basic stuff to an expert but a great learning experience for someone like myself who, despite regular visits since 1981, has only recently begun to appreciate more fully where the Germans actually were! Moving on we stop momentarily at the edge of a neighbouring field for Alan to pick up a shrapnel ball which he presents as a souvenir to a South African couple here in search of their ancestors. We'll keep running into these South Africans during the course of the afternoon; a common experience on the Somme, where there's a logical order to visiting the main sites. It's also one of the beauties of this kind of visit. You can strike up transitory acquaintanceships through a shared interest. They seldom last, but are in no way diminished by their brevity. Also you escape the dreaded "Oh, do pop in and see us if ever you're up our way" problem further down the line when the faces at the door are just a hazy, vaguely pleasant, memory from another time, another place!

Ending up at the memorial to Nine Brave Men at Bazentin-le-Petit is an appropriate way to complete our day's

Nine Brave Men at Bazentin

exploration as Alan was one of the team of Royal Engineers tasked with restoring it in the early 1970s.

Our third and last full day in Picardy promises to be a busy one and so next morning we're up early and off on the road towards Péronne. All of our work today is concerned with gathering photographic evidence for use on my website. The tiny village of Belloy-En-Santerre provides photos relating to the American poet, Alan Seeger, while Marteville and Roisel, situated among the very atmospheric *étangs* (ponds) of the upper Somme, are connected to the story of John Crawford Buchan, VC, who came from a house near to where I live in Scotland. Photo shoot completed, we travel back to the Albert-Bapaume area via Péronne where a blast, in the form of a *friterie* down by a little river, comes right out of the past to hit the old nostalgia button. Once, many years ago, we stopped here at the picnic tables, only then we were not alone. Instead we had 48 teenagers and a bus driver for luncheon companions, not to mention the ducks.

Memories of days long gone are understandably never far away on the Somme. What is surprising is their habit of sneaking up on you unexpectedly, hitting you somewhere behind the ear with a sock full of conflicting emotions and provoking a familiar stinging behind the eyes. Like the people being remembered, the memories themselves are old friends to be welcomed when they come knocking. Let them in before they grow cold.

Meanwhile there's more work to be done, beginning on a dusty back road leading from yesterday's Nine Brave Men at Bazentin to High Wood near Longueval. Tucked away on a little mound and shaded by a few trees is a Calvary atop a small memorial to Captain Wallace of the 10th Worcesters, killed on 22 July, 1916.

The inscription on the base asks us to pray for him and why not? He's just a name on a panel up at Thiepval. Somewhere close by is where he breathed his last and so it's here that his doting maiden aunt chose to erect a lasting monument to her beloved boy. Such "Crucifix Corners" at rural road junctions are

relatively common round here, like the two I've come across at Aveluy and Bazentin-le-Grand. The very well-known one at Aveluy is perhaps best appreciated if you keep your eyes trained heavenwards as the area round about is covered in litter left by what I hope are thoughtless local teenagers and not battlefield visitors.

The other at Bazentin is of fond memory, having provided me with a perfect shelter from a rainstorm when I was on a walking tour some years ago. There I sat, protected by the thick foliage from the deluge, contentedly munching some chocolate and waiting for the sun to shine once more. Very occasionally, a person can have a fleeting glimpse into what "peace" might really mean. That rainy interlude in the company of the shrapnel-riddled iron man on the cross was one of those occasions.

Finally we stop off for a quick photo at the memorial cairn to the Glasgow Highlanders with me demonstrating that I would probably not have made the minimum height of five feet seven inches even in boots. Thank God I didn't have to!

Next day our intention was to drive directly to Ypres. However a slight deviation due to roadworks took us close to an area scheduled for exploration later in the week. So, itinerary swiftly adapted, we detour through the farmlands of French Flanders to visit Albert Ball, VC, and the new cemetery at Fromelles.

Though Albert's story is very well known to aviation enthusiasts, I'm going to retell it anyway, hopefully with some new insights and reflections, in a future chapter. Suffice to say for the present, in taking the required photos my intrepid assistant, the wife(!), spared herself no discomfort even to the extent of trudging across a ploughed field to the crash site while the farmer was slinging pig slurry hither and thither. She got her pictures and I got a bill for a new pair of trainers.

Fromelles is a small town near Armentieres which until recently was visited only by those people interested in the disastrous battle fought there in 1916. Many of these visitors were Australians coming to see the ground on which so many of their countrymen had died. Since 2010, however, Fromelles has been subjected to the scrutiny of the world's media due to the discovery of hitherto unknown mass graves containing the bodies of some of these Aussie troops. The story of the archaeological dig and the subsequent reburial of these men is fully recounted in *Remembering Fromelles* by Julie Summers, available from the CWGC. While you're waiting for your order to be processed, a photo is below to whet your appetite.

Detour over, it's off to Ypres with the knowledge that good times lie ahead despite the tragic burden of history that

The new Australian cemetery at Fromelles

attaches itself to the town. No less a figure than Winston Churchill declared that "a more sacred place for the British race does not exist in the world". And he would know, having done some time in the hell that was the Salient. Today, though, it's a pleasant Flemish town with a fine main square, an abundance of cafes and inhabitants who know even better than those on the Somme how to turn the past into tourist gold.

A visit to the Ypres Saturday market on the Square provides enough fresh bread, cheese, fruit and chocolate to satisfy the keenest of appetites. In the peace of a warm Flanders day, a picnic lunch on the battlefields is surely one of life's greatest pleasures especially when shared with a congenial companion.

Now that continental markets regularly visit Britain, the one in Ypres is perhaps not so much of the novelty it once was, though it still contains some surprises. For example, I can't recall a stall in the UK where the local priest sells religious relics and candles and seems to do quite well out of the trade. Or where live rabbits are sold, but not for pets...

Our last two days were taken up with visits to old haunts like Toc-H in Poperinghe, and to such "newcomers" as the very effective visitors' centres at Langemark German Cemetery and up at Tyne Cot.

On our final day we went in search of some enlightenment on the very thorny subject of Flemish nationalism. At Houthulst Belgian Cemetery we couldn't find any raven crested headstones, apparently the sign of a nationalist burial, though we were reminded there of the unwanted legacy of the Great War. From time to time explosions shattered the silence as the Belgian military

continued their apparently endless job of disposing of the Iron Harvest in the nearby Houthulst Forest.

Dixmude on the other hand was more revealing, intimidating even. Redolent of the dark deeds of the past, a festering sense of injustice today pervades every corner of the massive *IJertoren* (Yser Tower) where a rather questionable "PAX" is carved in massive letters of stone on the stump of the original which was blown up "by unknown people" in 1946.

Finally we went on an unproductive trundle round Pervyse on the trail of the delightfully named Elsie Knocker and her companion, Mairi Chisholm, who, unable to get to the Front with the British, volunteered instead to nurse for the Belgians becoming in the process the legendary "Angels of Pervyse". Unfortunately, though they are fondly remembered, no trace of their adventures appears to have survived in the town.

Expedition over, the ferry glides out into the grey North Sea while we watch the white beach huts at Zeebrugge melting into the early evening twilight. From the bar there drifts a melody from the past. "Roses of Picardy" can still pluck at the old heartstrings especially when imaginary ghosts in khaki take up the refrain. Tomorrow we'll be back home but they never will be.

CHAPTER 9

THE SHORT BUT EVENTFUL LIFE OF ALBERT BALL, VC

I SUPPOSE all that's to be said about the life and career of Albert Ball VC has already been said. Done to death even, if I may be excused such an execrable pun. After all, he was just 20 in 1917 when his luck ran out over the muddy fields of French Flanders.

However, I'm going to have a crack at the subject in the hope that my recent research can add a little to what already exists. Now, where to begin? The houses where Albert lived in Nottingham, his home town, might be as good a starting point as any.

There seems to be a bit of confusion regarding the dwelling in which Albert was born on 14 August, 1896, apparently 301 Lenton Boulevard. Both of his recent biographers, Chaz Bowyer in 1994 and Colin Pengelly in 2010 (see bibliography), agree on this and so there seems to be no mystery there. The difficulty arises in trying to trace the infant Ball's domicile today for photographic purposes. You see, Lenton Boulevard was later incorporated into Castle Boulevard for reasons, I guess, of civic orderliness. There remains today a terraced house of the correct period at Number 301, Castle Boulevard. However, is this the same number as in 1896? To muddy the water still further, Pengelly reveals that 301 Lenton Boulevard eventually became 245 Castle Boulevard. Unfortunately there's no trace of that number today, just some contemporary commercial property where it once stood.

32 Lenton Boulevard: the birthplace of Albert Ball

However, a definite light was shone on these apparent contradictions in an article in *The Lenton Listener*, the magazine of the Local History Society. In Issue 14, published in 1981, it was revealed by none other than Albert's older sister, Mrs Lois Anderson, that the address in Castle Boulevard was NOT her brother's birthplace. Instead the great event occurred at 32 Lenton Boulevard, now given over to student accommodation. In fact most of the properties on Lenton Boulevard have, over the years, been converted into flats, in the process of which standards have fallen away sadly from the solid respectability of Albert's day. Be that as it may, given the provenance provided by Lois, I submit that we can safely accept that this latter address is definitely where little Albert chewed on his first Farley's Rusk. Though many might disagree with this rather cavalier assumption of authenticity, it's the best I've been able to come up with. Thankfully no such doubt exists about the decidedly upmarket dwelling which Albert left to go to war and, ultimately, to die.

Sedgley House, Nottingham: Albert's family home

Sedgley House is still there at 43 Lenton Road in the prestigious Park District of Nottingham, high on a rise overlooking the canal. Purchased by Albert's father, also Albert Ball, in early 1900 the house represented a significant move upward on Nottingham's social ladder. Though Albert Senior began his working life "in trade" in his father's plumbing business, he rapidly progressed through a mixture of diligence and opportunism to the pinnacle of the booming local property market. As a result he became not only wealthy but also respected enough to be elected Mayor of the city, not just once but four times, and to be elevated to a knighthood in 1924. In their home up near the Castle, his wife, Harriet, and the children – Lois, Albert and the youngest, Cyril – led a privileged, one might even say idyllic, life high above and a world away from the less salubrious parts of the city below.

As Chaz Bowyer, Albert's first "modern" biographer, indicates, "All three children benefited from the love and indulgence of a close-knit family life". Father Albert, though a tiger in commerce was, apparently, more of a pussy cat with his offspring, while Harriet was a loving mother totally devoted to their welfare. In return, the Ball parents received back the love and respect of their children, proof of which can be seen in Albert's letters home from the Western Front. Cocooned in apparent happiness, Albert was able to grow into a fine, if short, physical specimen, always on the lookout for fresh adventures. One of these youthful exploits reveals both his courage, or foolhardiness, and a very good head for heights, both desirable attributes for an aspiring fighter pilot. He celebrated his sixteenth birthday by accompanying a local steeplejack to the top of a factory chimney, a feat which, apparently, left him completely unfazed.

Albert's great interest in machines and electricity was also encouraged by his father providing him with that object of so many boys' dreams, a shed of his own. There Albert built radio and Morse equipment and even succeeded in reconstructing clapped-out petrol engines on his workbench, skills which would come in very handy as he sought perfection for his planes on the airfields of France. Young Ball also refined his skill as a marksman by blasting off with a handgun at various targets in the grounds of Sedgley. (Just imagine, dear reader, where such an exercise would land you in Nottingham today. A swoop by an emergency response team and a lengthy spell at Her Majesty's Pleasure, perhaps? Ah, the good old days...) With the benefit of hindsight, these youthful pursuits seem to lend a kind of inevitability to Albert's final destination, the cockpit of a fighter plane. However, as all this play and no work might make a rather dim boy, Albert's schooling was not going to be neglected.

To maintain the family's growing social status, Father deemed it necessary that the siblings should acquire that prerequisite of gentrified ambition, a good education. For Albert, this meant a scholastic journey from Lenton Church School via Grantham Grammar and Nottingham High to the more rarefied atmosphere of Trent College in nearby Long Eaton where he pitched up as a boarder in 1910.

Trent College today is a very upmarket co-educational fee-paying school with several impressive new structures no doubt endowed by grateful alumni. Fortunately for the purposes of this current project, it still maintains those buildings which would have been familiar to Albert. When our hero arrived there he was coming to what the English refer to as "a minor public school". To any American readers, this statement might come as a surprise. "Minor" Trent might

The Chapel at Trent College

have been; it most certainly was not "public". Only a select number of pupils (boys only then) would have been permitted to enter its portals, their admission determined either by academic brilliance (a few) or the ability to pay (the majority). In fact it was and remains a strictly private establishment.

Established in 1868 with the motto "Manners Makyth Man" and based on the tenets of the Church of England, it was by 1910 a Spartan establishment embracing the then popular notion of muscular Christianity. It might well be an understatement to describe Albert's Trent experience as "character forming". Cold baths in the morning and little or no heating would certainly have jolted him out of his previous comfortable existence at Sedgley. As was common practice, the boys followed a programme of strict discipline and exhausting exercise, presumably designed to suppress their adolescent sex drives. Such a regime did not always sit comfortably with Albert and it is at Trent that we first glimpse that resentment he would feel at what he perceived to be injustices, especially when they were engendered by the stupidity of those in charge of his destiny. One story recounted by both Bowyer and Pengelly involves Albert running away to sea after some run-in with authority at school. Apparently he ended up covered in coal dust in the engine room of a steamer outgoing from the port of Liverpool. Though there appears to be some doubt as to the authenticity of this tale, it is indicative that Albert was at least considered to be capable of such an act of rebellion, a refreshing thought given the prevailing stiff upper lip ethos of the time. Eventually, however, Albert seems to have fitted in reasonably well at Trent even to the extent of professing in one of his many letters home "a great love for my school". What then, if anything did Albert get from his schooling? Well, quite a lot it seems.

It gave a lad, described by aviation historian Peter Hart as "academically undistinguished", a chance to develop those skills which he undoubtedly possessed. He followed his mechanical inclinations to such an extent that, by 1912, he was professing a strong desire to go into electrical engineering on leaving school. Realising that he lacked the theoretical knowledge necessary to fulfil this ambition and showing a maturity beyond his years, Albert really buckled down, taking an extra year to make up for his previous shortcomings in mathematics and technical drawing. In what little spare time remained, he continued those hobbies of carpentry and photography begun in the shed at Sedgley and even revealed a hitherto unknown artistic side by learning to play the violin, an instrument to which he would later turn in times of stress. In addition to all this, his spell in the Officers' Training Corps at Trent, though at first going somewhat against his natural grain, gave him a sense of military discipline. This OTC experience would be of paramount importance to Albert's future, given his tendency occasionally to stand up to higher authority. It would also provide him with a fast track to promotion once he had taken the King's Shilling.

Though Albert was not always at ease at Trent, often preferring his own company, the school undoubtedly had a profound effect on him and, by the time he left aged 17 in 1913, many of the beliefs and traits of character which he would carry with him to the grave were firmly in place. Prominent among these were the aforementioned resentment of strict discipline, a keen sense of what he perceived to be injustice, and – above all – intense loyalty to family, school and, ultimately, country.

As Albert strode through Trent's gates at the end of the summer term in 1913 he presented a not unpleasing figure. A strong, stocky lad of five foot six inches, he was ready to take on the world outside – on his own terms, of course. He also had a clear idea, unusual in one so young, of the direction in which he was going. In the first instance, that was back along the road to Nottingham and the bosom of his family.

Not one to let the grass grow under his feet, Albert immediately set about getting himself a job, or at least his Dad did. Using his considerable influence, Mr Ball arranged for his son to be taken on by an electrical engineering firm in Castle Boulevard to gain vital practical experience. And that might have been that. Albert would follow his father up the ladder to commercial success and eventual civic honours. Unfortunately an assassination in middle Europe was going to put paid to all their dreams and schemes. Just over a year into his industrial apprenticeship, Albert put everything on hold to respond to his country's call to arms. On the 21st of September, 1914, Albert Ball, civilian, became Private Albert Ball in the ranks of the Robin Hood Battalion of the Sherwood Foresters.

From the very beginning of his military career, Albert's potential was spotted and he enjoyed a meteoric promotional boost, rising from humble private to 2nd Lieutenant within a month of his enlistment. All that bull and square-bashing in the OTC at Trent was now paying off, though Albert did not see it that way. He wanted to get to France in a hurry to grapple with his country's enemies but the very reason for his rapid promotion was to frustrate his immediate ambitions. His previous experience meant that he was just the man to train raw recruits and thus he was left, champing at the bit, in England. However, in 1915, Albert's military career was about to take a radical new turn. On a posting to Hendon, he discovered the joys of flight.

By leading an exhausting double life as army officer and personally financed trainee flier, Albert was awarded his pilot's licence in October, 1915. With his "ticket" to back him up, he could now transfer to the Royal Flying Corps (RFC) for pilot training in England. At last Albert had achieved his goal. He was on his way to the Front. Sporting his crisp new pilot's wings, he reported to Number 13 Squadron in France. It was the 18th of February, 1916, and Albert's war was about to begin in earnest.

For the first three months of his combat career, Albert was assigned to artillery spotting and photographic patrols piloting a two-seater BE.2c, described by Jack Herris in *Aircraft of World War I* as, "The reliable but vulnerable

BE.2c... ⟦which⟧... remained at the Front long after it was obsolete, suffering heavy losses to German fighters. Only their crews' courage enabled them to carry on".

Right from the beginning then, Albert was having to dip into a not-inexhaustible pot of bravery. However, relief was at hand. In May, all that Albert had been working towards came to fruition when he was assigned a much faster plane, the nippy Nieuport Scout. At last he was a real fighter pilot, ready to enter into aerial jousts with the enemy.

From April 1916 until his untimely but almost unavoidable death in May, 1917, Albert Ball wrought havoc among the squadrons of the Imperial German Air Service. Flying mainly in Nieuport Scouts, he engaged in 68 reported combats in which he notched up 44 'kills' – 43 aircraft and 1 observation balloon. Eleven of his last twelve combat victories came in SE5s, a plane which, though superior to the Nieuport, was not rated as highly by Ball.

Along the way to his date with death he accrued medals and public adulation. He became just what the proverbial doctor ordered, a much-needed national hero at a time when the country was reeling under the daily blows of ever-lengthening casualty lists. How then did Albert rise from being just an "average pupil" to the lofty status of Britain's leading ace in the space of fifteen months?

The BE.2c

The Nieuport Scout

From the very outset of his aviation career at Hendon, it was obvious that Albert relished flying despite, or maybe because of, the huge element of danger involved. The wobbly beginnings in training, which included crashing into some trees, he described as "a ripping time". But such simple enthusiasm is not going to get you to the top, though it helps. In fact, it was their very keenness that got many brave young pilots killed. Success in any field of endeavour depends on a number of vital ingredients among which are complete, almost blinkered, dedication plus attention to detail. Albert had those two in spades and, once he was in France, he went into overdrive.

Contemporary sources reveal that Albert was constantly "prowling around", watching what his mechanics, riggers and armourers were doing and generally checking that nothing, as far as he was concerned, was going to be left to chance. So keen was he, in fact, that he would get up before dawn to ensure that everything was to his satisfaction. The result was that he became as familiar with his machines as the members of his ground crew. All those hours pottering in his shed at Sedgley and the extra year at Trent were now beginning to pay major dividends. Content that his machine was in order, all that remained was for Albert to fly it. And how he flew it! Straight down the throat of the Hun.

The renowned writer, Cecil Lewis, who was a contemporary in the RFC, described Albert's combat style as follows.

"...His tactics were point blank, going right in, sometimes to within a few yards of the enemy, without the slightest hesitation..."

Preferring to attack the enemy from below, Albert would try for his opponent's blind spot and then, in his own chilling words, he would "hose him". As Peter Hart of the Imperial War Museum points out, these methods were extremely risky, frequently resulting in severe damage to his aircraft. Nevertheless Albert pressed on through the dark days of the Somme in 1916 and "Bloody April" in 1917 to rack up an impressive number of victories. No longer just an "average" flier, Ball had become, through hard work, experience and "suicidal bravery", a savage competitor to whom "superior numbers were as a red rag to the proverbial bull..." (Peter Hart).

I use the word "competitor" quite deliberately. Albert, like all great sportsmen, was fiercely competitive, becoming ever more obsessed with his "score" as the victory tally mounted. He was set upon becoming the ace of aces, especially if it meant one in the eye for his great French rival Georges Guynemer.

Gradually news of Ball's exploits filtered home and, by the time he went on leave late in 1916, he had become a real celebrity. The newspapers, hungry for any good news in that dreadful year of the Somme, grabbed Albert's coat tails and hung on like grim death. Albert was, quite simply, not only great copy but also "...a genuine hero..." who had established "...the true benchmark of courage" (Peter Hart).

It helped, of course, that he looked like a hero as he does in the following photo taken in early 1916.

He's got "the look", somewhat similar to Guy Gibson of Dambuster renown in World War II, whose exploits were equally used to cheer up a nation mired down in an apparently endless conflict. It now seems almost a paradox to observe that the nation's happiness level in both wars relied on killing people, combatants and non-combatants alike. Understandable, I suppose, given the military casualties on the Somme in 1916 and the civilian losses in the Blitz of the early 1940s. Be that as it may, Albert was

undoubtedly and deservedly England's darling in that far-off November of 1916. Girls adored him, matrons wanted to mother him and men admired him. Not bad going for a chap just turned 20.

It would have been excusable if all this fame had gone to Albert's head – but it didn't. According to Peter Hart, "...most found Ball an unassuming lad despite the fame and honours that had been showered upon him..." So "unassuming" in fact that he returned to France and to combat rather than remaining in England as an instructor. Life at the Front seems to have been preferable to Albert compared to the pressures of hero worship back home but there was a price, a huge price, to be paid for medals from the King and the Freedom of the City of Nottingham. And Albert would pay his bill in full. His letters home reveal just how "fagged" he was. Towards the end of the Somme campaign, the signs were beginning to show. "I was feeling very rotten and my nerves were poo-poo... Oh, I am feeling in the dumps..."

It's impossible to know whether or not this nervous exhaustion was exacerbated by Albert's 'loner' tendency. Throughout his flying career he preferred to shift for himself to the extent that he constructed a wooden shed (shades of Sedgley) on his main airfield in France. There he lived by himself, tending his little vegetable patch and spurning the chance to indulge in high jinks in the mess. Maybe he should have got out more, but hangovers would have interfered with his efficiency and close relationships in wartime usually lead to pain. Also he could play his violin without upsetting his colleagues.

Despite this horticultural therapy and regular fiddle playing, by April 1917 Albert was more than just "poo-poo";

he was nearing the end of his tether. By May 3 he revealed that he was "feeling so old" while in his last letter dated May 6 he informed his sister Lois that he had lost in a draw for leave. Characteristically, he brushed off any justifiable disappointment, resentment even, with the observation that it had been "a sporting chance". Next day, instead of being on a leave train for Boulogne, he had embarked on that last flight from which he never returned.

So that's that, I suppose – Albert, dead and buried (by the Germans incidentally). But who was it they were interring? Who was Albert Ball, VC? Intriguingly, the Albert revealed through his letters and the work of previous writers presents us with a series of paradoxes. A savage fighter with sympathy for his opponents. A hustling entrepreneur with plenty of ambition yet a traditional romantic with the girls. A bit of a rebel but, ultimately, a slave to duty.

We've already looked at Albert, the hunter-killer, but not at how he regarded his prey. The surviving letters in the Nottinghamshire Archives reveal a surprising attitude in one so devoted to killing the enemy. It quickly becomes obvious that, to Albert, his opponents were just ordinary Josefs doing their job, just as he was. A letter to his father at the height of the air battle over the Somme in July, 1916 shows us a young man far removed from the gung-ho hero created by the media. It's also very instructive in showing the gap that existed between the armchair generals in Blighty with those at the sharp end of battlefield reality.

> "You ask me to let the devils have it when I fight. Yes, I always let them have it when I can, but really I don't think of them as devils. I only scrap because it is my duty, but

I do not think anything bad about the Hun. He is just a good chap... trying to do his best. Nothing makes me feel more rotten than to see them go down, but you see it is either them or me, so I must do my best to make it a case of them."

Then this from a later missive:

"I feel so sorry for the chaps I have killed. Just imagine what their poor people must feel like... However it must be done..."

And, finally, just prior to his death:

"Oh! I do get tired of always living to kill and am really beginning to feel like a murderer..."

This obvious regret at having to kill shows a surprising maturity in one so young but I suppose boys grew up quickly in the cockpit of a Scout. To what extent this attitude prevailed generally among fighter pilots on the Western Front, I have no idea. However it certainly contrasts sharply with that of Edward 'Mick' Mannock, VC, another leading British ace, who, when apprised of the death of the fabled Red Baron, Manfred von Richthofen, observed, "I hope he roasted the whole way down..."

Ironically, it would be Mannock who was eventually "roasted", not the Baron.

Manfred von Richthofen

Peter Hart's research has uncovered evidence that a vestige of that fabled chivalry of old survived in the skies of France even if there was precious little in the mud below. For example, having engaged in a furious dogfight Albert found that not only he but also his opponent had exhausted their ammunition at which point "...we both burst out laughing... it was so ridiculous. We flew side-by-side laughing at each other for a few seconds and then waved adieu... He was a real sport that Hun."

In the final analysis, however, Albert knew that he was there to do a job, reducing the number of Germans flying about over France. He was also fully aware that his was a dirty job but someone had to do it. Duty, duty, always bloody duty.

However, away from all the guts and glory there existed another Albert Ball, Albert the young Lothario. He may have been a loner when surrounded by males, taciturn even, but put him in close proximity to a pretty female and he became positively garrulous.

Although it's likely that Albert would have been seen as "a bit of a catch" in his social circle in pre-war Nottingham, he doesn't seem to have had any "serious" relationships there. Nevertheless, as Colin Pengelly reveals, he did not lack for female companionship locally. However it was once he was in the RFC uniform, badged and booted and positively glowing with glamour, that he was on his way to the stars so far as girls were concerned.

From time to time he would have momentary misgivings about what he supposed were his philandering

Edward "Mick" Mannock, VC

ways. During these brief bouts of guilt he would unburden himself to his family, especially his father, in his letters home. On his 19th birthday, for example, he owns up to a positive charge sheet of romantic banditry. Beginning with "a ripping little girl" whom he is leading on with no "genuine" intentions, he is overcome with apparent remorse.

> "Now I look back on the last two years and see what a rotter I have been. I have fooled two girls that you know of, and, of course, I have made heaps of other girls think I liked them that you didn't know of. I really do feel a bit of a rotter but I really mean to stop now... I will try."

Sure, Albert, sure...
What are we to make of this "rotter" Albert, especially in light of these further revelations?

> "Really I cannot say what a job it is for me to be satisfied with just one girl, but it is a huge job..."

While, in reply to his father's remonstrations with regard to his behaviour over Yuletide, 1915, when he went out with "a few girl friends" in Nottingham while at the same time professing great love for another, "special" girl, we find:

> "Do please remember that it was Xmas time, also no one was at home... Don't forget that I am not exactly an Angel..."

At first glance it would appear that Albert had been cutting a swathe of sexual voracity across the Midlands and south of England. More realistically perhaps, he just liked female company and basking in the praise offered by impressionable young girls. What evidence can I offer for this interpretation? None at all, just a feeling that Albert was one of those for whom the thrill of the chase was as important as the end result. Much like he flew in fact. However, in May 2017, an article in the *Nottingham Post* threw up some very interesting information regarding our Albert's love life. His great niece, Mrs Vanda Day and her husband, Gordon, revealed for the first time the contents of Albert Ball's diaries which had been returned to the family shortly after his death. Among the entries were ones that had been erased, probably by Albert's father "to protect the family's reputation or perhaps to keep such details from his devoted mother". What were these "details" that Dad was so eager to suppress? After painstaking deciphering by Vanda and Gordon the erasures emerge as nothing less than "notes about various nights... spent in the best hotels, occasionally in the company of young ladies". Whether activities progressed any further than the downstairs restaurant we shall never know, but the suggestion is certainly there. I suppose it ain't nobody's business but the Balls', but in these days of tabloid prurience it's certainly intriguing.

The "special girl" referred to above whom Albert had "betrayed" at Xmas time, 1915, was his first serious girlfriend, Thelma Starr, known to Albert as "Pup" or "Tec" and, eventually and almost unbelievably, "Nipper".

This bestowing of incredibly twee nicknames is definitely Albert's most annoying trait and suggests, to me at least, in its childish naivety that his relationships with the girls were essentially of an "innocent" variety.

Thelma was the daughter of a manufacturer of domestic pots in Nottingham. Aged only about 14 and looking considerably younger with white ankle socks and pigtails, it's not surprising that Albert's family was never happy about this relationship. Whether for social reasons or because of her age, they constantly tried to get Albert to give "Tec" up which predictably he refused to do until, that is, the end of 1916 when she seems to have met someone else, presumably a chap who didn't call her daft names.

Never short of female company, Albert immediately declared himself to be in love with Dollie about whom nothing is known except for the fact that she was soon discarded for the latest model in March, 1917.

Flora Young was, apparently, the love of Albert's young life, given his rather elastic interpretation of the meaning of the word "love". She was certainly the most "suitable" of his long list of girlfriends – own car, well-off and pretty. She was also at 18 quite a mature addition to Albert's harem. Given his predilection for nicknames and fast working, it should come as no surprise that Flora swiftly became "Bobs" and the subject of another whirlwind onslaught. From an initial spin in Albert's plane on the 24th of March they had progressed to the position of "unofficial engagement" by the time he left for France in late April. In place of a ring he gave her a gold identity bracelet. Bobs would never see Albert again.

Combine Albert's bravery with his intense desire to be the ace of aces, add his highly individual tactics and a definite touch of battle fatigue to the mix and Albert's death seems, in retrospect, inevitable. Taking off in the early evening of May

7, 1917, he was piloting an SE.5, an excellent aeroplane but not his machine of choice. When the flight he was leading was attacked by five Albatros D.3s, Albert engaged in a brief skirmish during which he forced down Lothar von Richthofen, younger brother of you-know-who. Flying into heavy cloud, it would appear that Albert, despite his experience, became disorientated. Emerging from the cloud upside down and at too low an altitude to recover, he ploughed into farmland near Annouellin. He didn't stand a chance and died shortly afterwards in the arms of a young French woman. The prayer book Bobs had given Albert, presumably as a token of her love, was found on his broken body. It was all over – no more nicknames, no more flirtations, no more anything.

Albert was buried with full military honours by the Germans in their graveyard at Annouellin where he lies to this day, a lone Englishman surrounded by his former enemies.

A more appropriate ending could not have been devised by the kitschiest of screenwriters.

For Albert's contemporaries, the most immediate effect of his death was a temporary blip in the general morale of the RFC. However there would be precious little time for mourning – staying alive was a more pressing priority. But there was another consequence to Albert's death, one that has nothing to do with rationality.

Peter Hart reveals that an almost cult-like belief arose concerning the circumstances of his final flight.

> "The death of a great ace... often became enshrouded in as much mystery as the demise of a medieval saint. The fact that Ball was last seen flying into an ominous thundercloud only added to the slightly Arthurian nature of the reports of his death."

Despite the fact that Albert was firmly planted six feet under the turf of France, a belief persisted among some impressionable souls that he would return some day to pick up the torch once more like a latter-day Sir Francis Drake responding to the call of his Drum. All baloney, of course, but there was a lot of that particular sausage

around at the time, understandable I suppose given the almost surreal nature of the casualty lists. Even the inscription on his grave lends some support to this view. "Fighting Gloriously", Albert didn't die; instead he "Passed Over".

Back home the news of his death shattered his mother. She kept his room at Sedgley exactly as Albert had left it and so it remained until her own death in 1931. His father assuaged his grief in more practical ways by erecting a marker, which continues to survive the ravages of time and pig dung, on the approximate site of Albert's death and commissioning an impressive tombstone in the German cemetery in Annouellin.

In fact, Albert Senior seems to have been made of some pretty stern stuff. He soldiered on, becoming Lord Mayor of Nottingham yet again, receiving a knighthood and even finding the energy to remarry before his eventual demise in 1946 aged 83. His son would, I think, have been proud of him.

Albert's Crash Site Memorial (with muck spreader...)

Albert is remembered in a variety of ways in the Nottingham area. At Trent College there is a portrait and a propeller blade while in the city itself there is a fine memorial up at the Castle where he forever gazes skywards.

Also at the Castle, in the Sherwood Foresters' Regimental Museum there is an impressive display of relics and medals. Certainly the most practical legacy of his death locally is the Albert Ball Memorial Homes in Lenton just down from the church where the family worshipped. These houses were presented to the parish by Mr and Mrs Ball to be occupied by the widows and mothers of Lenton men who had been killed in action. They stand there today, a reminder that sometimes good can come out of tragedy.

Albert Ball College, Annouellin
(Perhaps a man doesn't always die when he stops breathing)

The greatest tribute to Albert however exists not in Nottingham but back in Annouellin in France. There the local secondary school is "Albert Ball College", a name chosen by the pupils themselves relatively recently.

When I began this chapter, it was with the feeling that it would all be done and dusted in the space of a couple of pages and a few photos. Yet here I am, around 6000 words later, still searching for the essence of Albert and finding only paradoxes.

He was devoted to his family, yet not above challenging his father from time to time. Devoted to his country yet a bit of a rebel. As keen as his father on making money, even to the extent of flogging cars and motorcycles to his RFC companions, yet also a hopeless romantic. Polite and affable yet a loner at heart. The terror of the skies and yet a deeply religious boy with a conscience about killing. A national hero, idolised wherever he went, yet innately modest.

Contradictions everywhere. So what certainties are we left with? Simply this one – Albert was a 100% genuine hero.

But the following words with which he closed one of his last letters to his family perhaps show us the real Albert Ball and what might have been.

"Tons of Love,
Albert"

* * *

Albert's Medals

- Military Cross: Gazetted 27 July, 1916
- Distinguished Service Order (DSO): Gazetted 22 September, 1916
- Bar to DSO: Gazetted 22 September, 1916
- Bar #2 to DSO: Gazetted 25 November, 1916
  (Thus Albert became the first triple DSO recipient.)
- Russian Order of St George: Gazetted 16 February, 1917
- French Legion d'Honneur: Gazetted 2 June, 1917 (Posthumous)
- The Victoria Cross: Gazetted 8 June, 1917 (Posthumous)

Not a bad haul for a little lad from Nottingham!

"LET RIGHT BE DONE!" THE WINSLOW BOY

FIRST let me say that it was appropriate that I first penned this chapter in 2011, the Terence Rattigan Centenary Year. Not only was Rattigan one of Britain's most prolific playwrights/screenwriters from the 1930s to 1960s, but his works were also hugely popular during that period. His greatest success was with *The Winslow Boy*, first produced on stage in 1946 and then in cinematic versions, first in 1948 and then, posthumously and probably definitively, in 1999. And it is with *The Winslow Boy* that a Great War connection arises, as the plot was based on the real-life *cause célèbre* occasioned by the unjust treatment of George Archer-Shee.

Archer-Shee was 13 in 1908 and a cadet at the Admiralty's Osbourne Naval College when he was accused of stealing a five shilling (25 pence) postal order from one of his classmates. (For my younger readers, five bob would have bought a lot of buns at the tuck shop in 1908.) The College/Admiralty summarily expelled George and that, for them, was that. However they had failed to take into account the boy's father, Martin, a comfortably fixed Liverpool bank manager who believed his son to be innocent and was willing to go to the ends of, if not the earth, at least the family's finances in pursuit of that belief. It is also possible that the College's swift dismissal of his son persuaded Martin, a devout Catholic, that religious prejudice might well have played a part in their decision as there were other suspects in the frame. So in order to defuse any such suspicions, Martin, in a PR masterstroke, engaged Sir Edward Carson, KC, the darling of the Ulster Protestants, to seek justice for his boy.

In his crusade for a review of the decision to expel George, Carson found his path bestrewn with obstacles judiciously placed in the way of truth by the Lords of the Admiralty who were behaving with the total inflexibility that typifies Establishment behaviour when forced on to the back foot. But Carson was not to be turned aside. Doggedly and brilliantly he fought his corner until, having exhausted all reasonable possibilities, he was forced to turn to the ancient device of a Petition of Right to none other than the Admiralty's boss, King Edward VII himself. When the King appended the words "Let Right Be Done" to the Petition, Carson could at last proceed with a suit against the College.

On July 30, 1910, amid scenes of wild excitement both in the courtroom and outside on the streets of the capital, the Admiralty was forced to accept that George Archer-Shee had indeed been wrongfully dismissed from the College. At long last, justice, albeit grudgingly, had been done.

On the happy side, Martin Archer-Shee, near bankruptcy due to his quest to clear his son's name, received substantial compensation and full legal costs. George, the "cause" of all the furore, went off to complete his education at

Stonyhurst College, the great Catholic public school in Lancashire.

On the not so happy side, in fact a complete downer, Lieutenant George Archer-Shee of the South Staffordshire Regiment, our Winslow Boy, was killed in action on October 31, 1914, during the First Battle of Ypres. With no known grave, his name is commemorated on Panel 35/37 of the Menin Gate Memorial to the Missing of the Ypres Salient. He is not alone. He has the company of 54,895 other lost boys. One of them, "Teddy" Robinson, was Sir Edward Carson's nephew and a fellow subaltern in the South Staffs. Killed just four days before George, Teddy is there sharing the panel with the Winslow Boy, just as his uncle had once shared a courtroom with him.

As the years went by, the Archer-Schee case became almost a folk memory but with enough life left in it to stir high emotion. It was practically demanding to be dramatised. "All" the prospective playwright had to do was to allow time to remove any cause for litigation, compress the timescale and then exercise a little dramatic licence, like changing the protagonist's name from Archer-Shee to Winslow. By 1945 a war-weary British public was ready for just such a work, far removed from the nightmare they'd just experienced, and Terence Rattigan was just the man to give it to them. His "drama of injustice and of a little man's dedication to setting things right" (Rattigan) struck just the right chord with audiences in 1946. It can still pluck a few heartstrings today.

Given what was to come in British theatre in the 1950s and, especially, the 60s, it is perhaps worth considering the following. With *The Winslow Boy*, Rattigan delivered a quieter but no less effective blow against the Establishment

SOUTH STAFFORDSHIRE REGT.

		BLA
J.	MAJOR	SERJEANT	BL/
	LODER-SYMONDS J. F.	DUFFIELD J. H.	BO
P. A.		DUNN A.	BO
	CAPTAIN	DYER W.	BO
	DUNLOP J. S. S.	HALL G. H.	BO
	POWELL H. M.	JONES A. C.	BR.
V	C.VALLENTIN J. F.	MITCHELL W. E.	ER
		MORLING C. D.	BR
	LIEUTENANT	PURCHASE E.	BF
	ARCHER-SHEE G.	SIMONS A.	BF
	CROUSAZ C. F.	SMITH J.	BF
	FITZPATRICK D. T. F.	STANYARD E. L.	BF
O AS	HOLMES F. L.	TAYLOR W.	BF
1 H.	HUME C. G.	THORPE J. H.	B
	MOOR-RAFORD L. C.	UNDERHILL C. V.	B
/. C.	ROBINSON F. E.		B
		LANCE SERJEANT	B
	SECOND LIEUT.	BAKER J.	E
	LEWIS G. A. D.	BRATT D.	(
	SCOTT B. J. H.	JEFFERIES T.	(

Menin Gate: George Archer-Shee appears as the fifth name down the left-hand column

equal to anything that followed from the Angry Young Men who succeeded him.

It might appear that this tale has had only a tenuous connection to the overlying theme of this book, the Great War. But its shadow is there all the time. The waste, the terrible waste. All that effort, all that devotion, all that moral courage expended in an English court room in 1910 to prove the innocence of a young boy, all wiped out in the Flanders clay four years later.

There was no happy ending for the real Winslow Boy.

* * *

Postscript

As a result of this chapter originally appearing on my website I received a most interesting e-mail from Mike Newell, who can claim a connection to *The Winslow Boy* which is second to none. He is the original "Winslow Boy" of the theatre.

Impressed by Mike's performance in a previous play at the Lyric Theatre in London, Terence Rattigan cast him in the title role of his new work in 1946. There Mike remained for the entire London run before going on to further success in the role on Broadway. In fact, he was the only cast member to last for the entire three year run of 1048 performances. Unfortunately, due to contractual commitments he was unable to take part in the 1948 film. Post-Winslow Boy, Mike went on to have a very fulfilling career on the stage, in films and on TV and now lives in happy but very active retirement in Virginia.

It's nice to know that the theatrical Winslow Boy at least has survived to a grand old age, unlike his real-life counterpart who is now just an interesting, tragic footnote in the history of the Great War.

CHAPTER 11

ON THE WARPATH

THE roar of souped-up engines and the whistles of the marshals split the balmy autumn air of a Flanders afternoon. Low slung Citroens and Peugeots are hurtling round the narrow country lanes in one of those mad rallies so beloved of the otherwise stolid Flemish. There seems to be absolutely no chance of crossing the narrow strip of road separating me from Passchendaele New British Cemetery and the grave of Alex Decoteau. Then an engine stalls on the starting grid and I'm off, scuttling across the temporary racetrack and through the graveyard gate before blue exhaust fumes and burning rubber signal that the next session of motor mayhem is under way.

Close to where the cemetery is located today, a wild Canadian, "Hoodoo" Kinross, had charged across a muddy field at the end of October, 1917, *en route* to winning the Victoria Cross. Against all the odds, he survived (see Chapter 5). Alex Decoteau, a fellow Canadian soldier, would not be so lucky. Nothing unusual, I suppose, given the scale of the slaughter. Just another body among thousands of other Canadian dead, all of them worthy of remembrance in one

way or another. Why then should Alex deserve more than just a passing mention?

First and foremost, Alex was a Native Canadian, a Cree Indian, born on the reservation at Battleford, Saskatchewan in 1887, "Decoteau" probably being a French-Canadian version of the Indian "Dakota". However Alex is worth remembering for far more than his ethnic origins, interesting as they are.

Educated at the Battleford Industrial School, he proved himself adept at grasping any opportunity which came his way, particularly on the sports field. Though he was a gifted all-round athlete, it would be primarily as a runner that Alex would make his bid for lasting fame.

From the early 1900s, Alex stamped his authority on Canadian middle and long distance running, at first locally and then at a national level. In conjunction with his athletic success he was also ascending the socio-economic ladder. Moving in 1909 to Edmonton, Alberta, to live with his sister and brother-in-law, he was accepted as an officer by the Edmonton Police Force, a landmark achievement for a Native Canadian. Promoted to motorcycle cop, Alex became a popular figure round and about Edmonton, especially as his exploits on the running track began to be widely reported.

Competing in races ranging from one to ten miles, Alex established himself as one of the top Canadian distance runners. So successful was he that by 1912 he had reached the pinnacle of an athlete's career, Olympic selection. Chosen for the Canadian team to compete in the Stockholm Games, he fell short of doing himself justice in the 5000 metres due to an agonising attack of cramp mid-race. Nevertheless he acquitted himself well by gritting it out to finish eighth.

Returning to Edmonton, Alex's athletic success continued but, even more important for his long-term prospects, was his promotion to sergeant in the police department, in charge of a city station. By blazing a trail through the barriers of convention, Alex had, by 1914, become a role model for all young Canadians, regardless of race, and was well on his way to establishing a benchmark of excellence to which they could aspire. But there would be no more Olympic appearances or further promotion in the police department. Far away from the prairies, the outbreak of the Great War was to decide otherwise.

Alex enlisted, appropriately, in the 202nd Edmonton Sportsmen's Battalion in 1916, transferring later to the 49th Battalion of the Edmonton Regiment, "The Loyal Eddies", the outfit to which the aforementioned "Hoodoo" Kinross had signed up in the previous year. As the son of Peter Decoteau, a Cree warrior who had distinguished himself in the skirmish at Cut Knife Hill in 1885, it was now Alex's turn to show what he could do on the field of battle.

After the usual spell of training in England, during which time he continued to race successfully, Alex arrived in Belgium in the autumn of 1917 in time to do his bit for Canada and the Loyal Eddies. Unfortunately, Alex's "bit" was going to be done at Passchendaele, where so many young dreams were dashed to pieces. Though details of Alex's time in Flanders are sparse, what is without question is that he died, as a warrior should, on the field of battle, felled by a sniper's bullet on October 30, 1917 at the age of 29.

In the years to follow, most victims of the War were remembered only by their close relatives with "at each slow dusk a drawing down of blinds" and a name on a war memorial. Alex, however, would not fade so easily into the grey mists of the past.

Because of his origins on the reservation, his national fame as a runner and his local renown as a motorcycle policeman, his memory has been kept alive until the present day in his native Canada, a country which knows how to revere its veterans and its heroes. Likewise, in Flanders, Alex is not just a name on a headstone.

Back home Alex has been inducted into the Alberta Sports Hall of Fame, has had a play about his life performed and annual runs for youngsters organised in his name, while in Belgium in November 2007, the Alex Decoteau 10km race was inaugurated at Passchendaele close to where he now rests. And the commemorating of Alex shows no signs of abating. At the Edmonton Police Headquarters at the end of

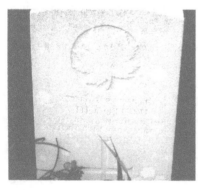

2010 a display of memorabilia pertaining to her uncle was unveiled by Izola Mottershead who has done so much to keep Alex's memory alive.

Perhaps the most poignant remembrance of all, however, was held in

1985 on the Red Pheasant Reservation where a traditional ceremony was performed to bring back Alex's spirit from Belgium for a proper Cree burial. Without this rite his ghost would have been condemned to wander the earth forever like the Flying Dutchman.

Hopefully Alex is now home for good among the folks, both Native Canadian and non-Indian alike, who care so deeply about him. His body may lie in Flanders fields but his spirit rests once more on the hunting grounds and in the lodges of his forefathers.

While he was in Belgium, Alex encountered Tom Longboat, a fellow Native Canadian athlete and soldier, but one whose life would take a markedly different turn from that of Alex.

Unlike Alex, who was a child of the Saskatchewan prairies, Thomas Charles Longboat was born in 1887 one thousand miles to the east on the Six Nations Reserve at Brantford, Ontario. He too was to develop into an ace long distance runner.

Competing as an amateur at first, Tom began racing in earnest in 1905 and by 1907 had become good enough to win the now legendary Boston Marathon in a record time. Expected to do well in the marathon at the 1908 London Olympics, Tom was bitterly disappointed, failing to finish the race. In this he was not alone – 50 percent of the field fell by the wayside in the uncharacteristic blistering heat. In addition, Tom's preparations for what was meant to be the race of his lifetime could not have been helped by an American attempt to ban him on the grounds that he was a "shamateur" who had accepted money prizes in previous races. This would not, I suppose, have been surprising, given Tom's less than silver spoon upbringing, a fact which set him apart from most of his fellow competitors, many of whom were gentleman athletes. Where they had rich daddies to support them, Tom had to rely on his own efforts to raise his eating money. So, all things considered, Tom's Olympic efforts, dropping out at the twenty mile marker after having been in second place for most of the race, might charitably be described as one of those "noble failures" which litter mankind's history. On a happier note, Tom got hitched to Lauretta Maracle in that same year, though this marriage was to have a truly bizarre ending.

Bitterly disappointed Tom might well have been, but he didn't have time to brood about London. In fact he soon bounced back. Since so many other fancied runners had also failed to finish, a rematch was run the same year in Madison Square Garden in New York and this was handily won by Tom. Turning pro in the aftermath, Tom was now legit and could race openly for cash. He didn't have long to wait for success.

By 1909 he had been crowned Professional Marathon Champion of the World and, though deeply disillusioned by being "sold" to an American promoter by his supposedly trustworthy manager, Tom just went on winning. However it was becoming obvious to sportswriters and fans alike that all might not be well with him. Enter the Demon Firewater, the downfall of so many sportsmen past and present especially those who rise from humble origins. By 1911 Tom had appeared in court on a drunkenness charge and the bottle was becoming rather too close a friend. Since he continued to compete with frequent success, it would appear that he was not an alcoholic as such, more of a binge drinker, able to stay

Ned Hanlon, Duncan Scholes, and Longboat of Toronto, Canada

off the stuff long enough to get the job done. So his life and career went on, his races against the great English runner, Alfred Shrubb, in particular attaining almost legendary status in the annals of athletics. In 1916, however, his running was to take on a new purpose.

In February of that year, Tom enlisted in the 107 Pioneer Battalion of the CEF where his talents were put to good use as a dispatch runner. He seems to have taken well to army life if the above photo of him negotiating the purchase of a newspaper from a French urchin is anything to go by.

Tom's role as a runner led to him being twice wounded. Curiously it was also reported that he had been killed in action, a mistake that was to have rather serious consequences for his marriage. Returning home after the War, Tom had little left to smile about. Now over thirty years of age, his athletics career was finished, as was his marriage to Lauretta. Perhaps understandably, going on the available information about Tom's supposed demise, she'd remarried in 1918. Frustratingly, for how long Tom remained officially "dead" I just don't know, nor do I have any idea about the legal implications of his period in limbo. It sure would make the basis for a good drama though.

With his marriage having gone west and with running no longer an option, Tom had to make a life for himself. Settling in Toronto with a new wife, Martha, with whom he had four children, he worked for the city as a garbage collector until 1944 when he retired back to the Six Nations Reserve. He died there in 1949, aged just 61, of pneumonia, his condition probably exacerbated by those twin nemeses, depression and drink. It was a less than glorious but probably predictable exit for the man who had once been a shining star in the athletics firmament.

Tom was gone but, like Alex Decoteau, he has not been forgotten. The Tom Longboat Awards honour outstanding Native Canadian athletes while his name and

achievements are also commemorated by the annual Toronto Island 10 km race.

Comparing Tom and Alex Decoteau is perhaps inevitable given their common ethnicity, success as athletes and their roles as members of the Canadian Army. There, I think, the parallels end. Personally Alex and Tom were very different human beings. Alex was a man who succeeded by dint of hard work and dedication in his endeavours both on and off the athletics track while Tom was beginning to show the signs of burn-out well before the end of his sporting career. To say this is not to praise one and condemn the other. Who knows why the lives of men – and women – follow the paths they do? Maybe only the people themselves or their nearest and, hopefully, dearest can shed some light. When they are gone, only the cups and medals and a few fading photographs remain to remind us a little of who they once were.

Perhaps Louise Cuthand in her article "Tom Longboat: A Notable Indian Athlete" best sums up the influences which wounded Tom more deeply than the German bullets in Flanders.

"He died back on the Six Nations Reserve in 1949, a victim of his own talents, the rapaciousness of promoters, the short-lived worship of the public and his vulnerability to the corruptions of white society."

Brutally frank but probably true, Ms Cuthand's assessment is reinforced by the words of Tom's original trainer.

"If we could've kept him on the reservation and brought him out just to run, what he could've done would have been even more remarkable."

Alex and Tom were only two of more than 3500 soldiers of Native Canadian origin who served, and often died for, their country in the Great War. This figure is truly impressive when one considers that Native Canadians were exempt by treaty from any participation in foreign wars. Why then, did they choose the white man's path and volunteer? Perhaps Bucholz, Fields and Roach are right in their contention in *Native Americans and the Military* that it all comes down to "the proud warrior tradition". As Mike Mountain Horse of the Blood Band from Alberta and a veteran of the Great War remarked:

"The War proved that the fighting spirit of my tribe was not squelched through reservation life. When duty called, we were there and our people showed all the bravery of old."

Despite all the brickbats that fate and a sometimes forgetful or even hostile white majority could throw at them, the "Indians" were indeed "there".

But perhaps their most telling reason for risking life and limb in battle is a different way of looking at death – and life. Back in 1890, Chief Crowfoot of the Blackfoot had this to say when faced with his approaching death:

"What is life? It is the flash of the firefly in the night. It is the breath of the buffalo in the winter time. It is the little shadow that runs across the grass and loses itself in the sunset."

As John Keats once wrote about something else entirely, "...that is all ye know on earth, and all ye need to know".

* * *

Postscript

Now comes own up time! I am acutely aware that dealing with the subject of Native Canadians in the Great War or anywhere else can be fraught with controversy in these racially sensitive times, especially when the writer is no expert on the subject. For any mistakes or wrong assumptions I therefore offer my apologies to those whom my shortcomings might unintentionally have offended. However, I can assure all my readers that I undertook this chapter with the very best of motives. You see, it was all inspired by an autumnal moment of contemplation at the grave of Alex Decoteau. With the wind rustling through the trees I just could not ignore his call or, when I found him later, that of Tom Longboat. To me, they are both heroes.

CHAPTER 12

WEE COUNTY HEROES: CLACKMANNANSHIRE'S FOUR VCs

CLACKMANNANSHIRE lies towards the eastern end of the Central Scotland plain, bounded in the north by the Ochil Hills and to the south by the River Forth. Its main claim to fame in the past was its position as the smallest county in Britain, smaller even than Rutland in England. Its inhabitants still refer to it as "The Wee County", taking a kind of defiant pride in so doing.

"Wee" it might be, but there is nothing small about the deeds of four men who brought honour to their native heath by winning Britain's premier award for gallantry, the Victoria Cross: John McDermond, James Dalglish Pollock, James Lennox Dawson and John Crawford Buchan. Let us begin our narrative with John McDermond.

Unfortunately, little is known of McDermond's life, not surprising when one considers that he was probably born into poverty. He certainly died in that penurious state. In fact, that is just about all we know about him apart from the

account of his VC action in the Crimean War and the bare details of his Army career.

His birthplace is often misrepresented as Glasgow but he actually had his origins in Clackmannanshire. Just as frustrating, the most commonly quoted birth and death dates assigned to John are also in dispute. While most sources give his date of birth as 1832, it is more likely that it was 1828 and the year of his death 1866, not 1868. Why, you might well ask, should we go with these "revised" dates? The answer is that they are confirmed in McDermond's Army Discharge Papers held in the National Archive at Kew, and it is from this document that I have gleaned the following information.

John enlisted in the 47th Regiment of Foot at Glasgow on the 24th October, 1846, giving his age as 18, which would make the year of his birth 1828. Admittedly there is the possibility that John falsified his age to enter the Army to escape a life of poverty. He may have been born in 1832 but there is no trace of his birth either at Register House in Edinburgh or in the Clackmannanshire Parish Records, which would imply that it was never recorded, a common enough occurrence in the first half of the 19th century. His place of birth in his Army papers is given as "in or near the town of Clackmannan" and his civilian occupation as "labourer", probably a farm worker, a position close to the very bottom rung of the economic ladder. Faced with a future of unremitting and largely unrewarded toil, John scraped the mud from his boots and went off to join the soldier boys. Whatever his reason for enlisting, John McDermond, labourer, began a new life as Private 2040 McDermond on that October day in 1846. For the next sixteen years Clackmannan would be only a distant memory for John as he embarked upon his great adventure. And adventures he had aplenty.

His foreign postings included the Ionian Isles (Greece), Malta, Turkey, Gibraltar, Canada and, most significantly, the Crimea, a peninsula jutting out from Russia into the Black Sea. It was there during the Crimean War (Britain, France and Turkey versus the Russians) that John McDermond would rise above the common herd to become one of the heroes of the Empire.

At the Battle of Inkerman on November 5, 1854, Private McDermond plunged into a melee to rescue his commanding officer, Colonel Hay, who was on the ground, wounded and surrounded by a mob of Russians. Killing the very man who had wounded his colonel, McDermond, with the help of Captain Hugh Rowlands of the 41st (Welsh) Regiment of Foot, managed to drag the officer to the safety of the British lines. For this deed, McDermond was awarded the VC, the 37th of the campaign, and the only one to have been bestowed upon his regiment. The hero, who had been wounded during his rescue mission and then again later in the year at the Battle of the Alma, was shipped back home where he eventually received his medal in 1858.

John continued to serve with the 47th and would probably have remained with them for the rest of his working life but for a very unfortunate accident. In July, 1861, he injured his ankle while on board ship with his regiment *en route* to Canada. Whether due to neglect or just bad luck, his injury turned out to be serious enough for him to be repatriated to Chatham. There, the opinion of the Principal Medical Officer sealed John's fate:

> "Having examined Private John McDermond, I am of the opinion he is unfit for further service. Partial ankylosis R. ankle – is quite lame."

So that was it for John. Still a fine figure of a man on his discharge in July, 1862, at the age of 33 – five feet eight inches in height, with a fresh complexion, blue eyes and sandy hair – he faded back into the obscurity from whence he had arisen, discarded as unfit for purpose by a completely uncaring military. According to his death certificate, he returned to one of the few jobs open to an unskilled discharged soldier. Once again he was a labourer, forced to go back to the very job he'd joined up to escape. Given the fact that his injury had been sufficiently serious for him to be discharged from the Army, it's hard to see that his services with a pick and shovel would have been in much demand either. Whether they were or not didn't really matter as he would only have to bear his burden for another four years. He died in Glasgow on July 22, 1866, of typhus fever.

It might have been more fitting if his death certificate had attributed his demise to general despair and poverty caused by his premature dismissal from the Army and subsequent lack of support from a country which he'd served so well. His Army pension had been increased to one shilling per week just twelve days before his death. Taking this less than princely sum in conjunction with his annual £10 VC gratuity, it seems fair to surmise that John McDermond was not exactly living in the lap of luxury. It's sad but not surprising that his final resting place should be an unmarked grave in the paupers' plot in Woodside Cemetery, Paisley, Common Ground, Section 26.

Hopefully, any doubts about the location of McDermond's birthplace have now been put to rest and he can rightfully be claimed as the first of the Wee County VCs. However, one mystery still remains – the whereabouts of his medal. According to the medal expert, Iain Stewart, "...it hasn't been seen, sold, donated or loaned since he was invested with it on 12 March, 1858". It would be nice but highly unlikely to think that it rests with its rightful owner in that unmarked grave in Paisley.

No such mysteries are attached to the next two Clackmannanshire VCs. All the relevant information about their lives is fully documented from their births to their last resting places. And this information reveals some noteworthy coincidences. Not only did both come from the same small Clackmannanshire town but they were also related, won their medals on the same battlefield, Loos, within two weeks of each other and both, remarkably, survived the War.

One pace forward, James Dalglish Pollock and James Lennox Dawson, the fighting cousins of Tillicoultry!

James Dalglish Pollock, henceforth to be referred to in this narrative as simply "Pollock" for the sake of brevity, was born in the little burgh on June 3, 1890, at 24 Ochil Street. Nestling at the foot of the Ochil Hills, which provided both

Corporal JAMES D. POLLOCK, V.C.

water power and grazing for sheep, Tillicoultry was a "wool town".

Pollock's father, Hugh, was a foreman in one of the local mills and it was there that his son obtained employment in the warehouse and offices after his school days were over. An able lad, Pollock moved rapidly upwards in the textile industry working as a "rep" or commercial traveller. In that capacity he travelled extensively in France, Belgium and Holland, becoming fluent in the languages required to conduct the business of the firm. Pollock had certainly come a long way from his relatively humble beginnings in Ochil Street.

At the outbreak of the War he was in Paris from where he swiftly returned home to volunteer. Aware that his linguistic abilities could be of great use, he offered his services as a translator. However, in the time-honoured tradition of the British Army of finding round holes to force square pegs into rather than apply a bit of common sense, his offer was rejected and

Ochil Street, Tillicoultry, c.1900

he enlisted in the 5th Battalion of the Queen's Own Cameron Highlanders.

While at home, Pollock had been a member of the Territorial Army and so it isn't surprising that he was soon promoted to Corporal and sent out to France in March, 1915. On the 27th of September he found himself on the battlefield near the coalmining town of Loos in northern France. The day that would define the rest of his life had arrived.

The Hohenzollern Redoubt was a formidable German defensive position set amongst the spoil heaps of the Loos coalfield. It had been attacked previously by the 2nd Worcesters but their offensive had stalled by the 27th, pinned down by German grenade throwers who were working their way up the charmingly-named Little Willie Trench. Seventy men of the Black Watch plus thirty Cameron Highlanders were sent to sort things out. Among them was 12087 Corporal J.D. Pollock, a specialist in the hurling of Mills

Bombs. What happened next is best left to the VC citation in the *London Gazette* of November 18, 1915:

> "For most conspicuous bravery near the Hohenzollern Redoubt on 27th September, 1915. At about 12 noon, when the enemy's bombers in superior numbers were successfully working up the Little Willie Trench towards the Hohenzollern Redoubt, Corporal Pollock... got out of the trench alone and walked along the top edge with the utmost coolness and disregard of danger and compelled the enemy's bombers to retire by bombing them from above. He was under heavy machine-gun fire the whole time but contrived to hold up the progress of the Germans for an hour when he was at length wounded."

The fact that he was "bombing them from above" meant that Pollock was dangerously exposed to enemy fire. Perhaps he was fortunate to get off with "just" a wounded arm. As he described the incident in a letter to his mother:

> "We got outside the parapet and crept along outside the trench and got a queer peppering but luck was with us... We crept on a bit closer and I got one of the Huns with my second bomb. I got another two with my third and I was about to fling a fourth when I got a bullet clean through my arm. This put an end to operations so far as I was

concerned, so I made all haste to get back to our lines. How I managed to get back safely was a miracle as bullets were whistling all around me but fortunately I was not once hit..."

Pollock's wound was a much coveted "Blighty One" and he was transferred to hospital in Dublin to recover, unaware that he was about to become public property.

On Saturday, December 4, 1915, Pollock went to Buckingham Palace to receive his Victoria Cross from King George the Fifth. One week later, on his return to his roots, the floodgates opened. Despite cold, wet weather, Tillicoultry was in festive mood for his homecoming. The station, draped in bunting, was thronged with the townsfolk. The local bigwigs formed a welcoming party on the station platform from where a procession set off through the town. Pollock's transport was by a horse drawn gun carriage accompanied by outriders provided by officers of the Royal Field Artillery while the band of the Royal Scots played, appropriately, "The March of the Cameron Men" and "See, The Conquering Hero Comes". Then at the Town Hall and to rapturous applause, Pollock received from Lord Mar, the Lord Lieutenant of the County, £70 and a gold watch.

Of course, as might be expected after all this bounty, the piper had to be paid and this Pollock did by appearing at three local schools, Tillicoultry, Coalsnaughton and Dollar Academy. The purpose of the hero's visits becomes quite clear when one considers Lord Mar's words at the Town Hall presentation:

"We are passing through anxious days... we have found it a tougher job than we expected..."

So Pollock's task was twofold. His very presence would act as a much needed morale booster while his celebrity status would hopefully encourage the youngsters to join up when they came of age. Lord Mar, like Lord Kitchener before him, was definitely thinking long term.

The visit to Dollar Academy was of special significance. The boys there gave Pollock a rousing reception and he signed autographs for the members of the school's Officer Training Corps. At the end, had he asked them to follow him to the Front, it seems likely that the entire school would have trooped after Pollock, VC, the Pied Piper of Tillicoultry. As it was, the eager would-be recruits had to content themselves with marching with their hero down to Dollar Station to catch the train for the five minute journey back to his home town.

Lest I've given the impression that Pollock was blindly exhorting the Dollar boys to join up when their time came, I should point out in fairness that he had, in his address, expressed the hope that the War would be over by then.

Faced with all this adulation, Pollock was probably glad to get away from his home area to the comparative calm of the officers' training school at Gailes in Ayrshire early in 1916, the Army's "reward" for his actions at the Hohenzollern Redoubt. It is there, on the windswept coast of the west of Scotland, that we shall leave James Dalglish Pollock, VC, for the present and turn our attention instead to Cousin Dawson.

James Lennox Dawson was brought into the world, as his cousin James Dalglish Pollock had been, by Dr Currie of Tillicoultry. Born at 05.30 on Christmas Day, 1891, Dawson was eighteen months younger than his fellow VC. In actual fact, the boys were only second cousins, as it was their fathers who were full cousins. Before moving in 1909 with his parents to Alloa, Dawson resided at 1 Hill Street, Tillicoultry, a house long since demolished. This shift in the Dawson abode was to be the source of some friendly rivalry in 1915 between the provosts of Alloa and Tillicoultry, both of whom were eager to claim James as their town's native son.

Dawson received his secondary education at Alloa Academy from where he went on to the University of Glasgow to study chemistry, a subject choice which would later prove to be most useful to him. In 1912 he was appointed to the post of science master at the Hill Trust School in the Govan district of Glasgow where he stayed until October, 1914, when he responded to his country's call to arms.

Although Dawson had enlisted originally in the Cameronians, by March, 1915, the Army, in one of its more rational moments, decided that it could make use of his qualifications and promoted him to Corporal in the Royal Engineers. There he joined 187 Company, one of the Special companies. "Special" indeed. These were the men who would respond in kind to the German use of poison gas, a weapon which the Hun had first released at the Second Battle of Ypres in April, 1915.

So it was that James Lennox Dawson found himself in September, 1915, not only on the same battlefield, Loos, as his cousin but also in the same area, facing the Hohenzollern Redoubt.

Just sixteen days after Pollock's exploits, it was Dawson's turn to win the Victoria Cross. Once again, let us turn to the columns of the *London Gazette*:

"For most conspicuous bravery and devotion to duty on 13th October, 1915, at Hohenzollern Redoubt. During a gas attack, when the trenches were full of men, he walked backwards and forwards along the parapet, fully exposed to very heavy fire, in order to be the better able to give directions to his own sappers, and to clear the infantry out of the sections of the trench that were full of gas. Finding three leaking gas cylinders, he rolled them some sixteen yards away from the trench, again under very heavy fire, and then fired rifle bullets into them to let the gas escape. There is no doubt that the cool gallantry of Corporal Dawson on this occasion saved many men from being gassed."

In a manner very reminiscent of his cousin, he had dared and survived.

Dawson received his medal from the King at Buckingham Palace on December 15, 1915. The fact that he was the only "Special" VC may point to the ambiguous position that the British took on the use of poison gas. They had made the usual big deal of "Hun frightfulness" after the Germans' initial use of it, but were more than willing to employ it themselves to achieve their own ends. Dawson himself felt compelled, in a speech to the pupils of Sunnyside School back in Alloa, to condemn the Germans' "dirty methods" while justifying Allied use of "any method at all" to get the job done. The Germans had started it, after all!

Much as we might today deplore our use of "the accessory", such doubt is a luxury only allowed to later generations safe from the slaughter of their sons and daughters; it certainly would have troubled the consciences of very few people in the dark days of 1915. Instead, the people back home longed for heroes and James Lennox Dawson fitted the bill perfectly.

The celebrations on Dawson's return rivalled in terms of warmth the ones accorded to Pollock just two weeks previously. He visited his old school in Govan, addressed cheering throngs of pupils in Clackmannanshire and was showered with tributes from local dignitaries at civic receptions.

In scenes presaging today's celebrity stake-outs by the tabloids, the Dawson family in Alloa was harried by reporters and cameramen from the national papers much to the shock of the more sedate local press, which described them ironically as "colleagues of the pencil and their allies of the camera – scribblers and snapshotters". One of these denizens of the lower depths even managed by subterfuge to gain access to the Dawson home.

The hero worship peaked on the 18th of December when huge crowds and the band of the Royal Engineers greeted the returning hero at Alloa Station from where he toured the town in an open carriage. 35 Paton Street, Alloa, besieged by well-wishers as well as the aforementioned "scribblers and snapshotters", was, for a short time, the most renowned address in Clackmannanshire. As a neighbour proudly declared, "Aren't we the grand street noo!"

Such rapturous receptions as those afforded Pollock and Dawson might easily have turned their heads but, remarkably, the lads kept themselves on an even keel. Once all the cheering had died down they just got on with the rest of their lives and careers. Pollock, as already stated, went to officer school in Ayrshire. Having completed his course, he returned to the front line later in 1916. His luck held until spring, 1917, when he lost the sight of his left eye at Arras. Invalided out of the Army with the rank of Captain, he worked for the Ministry of Munitions in France for a short while before coming back to Ayr where in 1919 he married a girl whom he'd met in 1916 while attending officers' school. A civilian once more, he returned to the textile industry where he forged a highly successful career. During the Second World War he served at home as a fulltime member of the Royal Observer Corps with, as might be expected, "distinction". He was still working at the age of 67 when, in May 1958, he died shortly after one of his frequent business trips to Canada. He is buried in his wife's family grave in Ayr Cemetery.

For James Lennox Dawson, like his cousin, there would be no immediate respite from his service career. He too returned to France. Wounded at the Battle of the Somme in 1916 he was shipped back to the UK where he remained until demobbed in 1919 with the rank of Major. He returned to the

University of Glasgow to extend his academic qualifications before returning to the Army in 1920, this time in the less dangerous ranks of the Army Education Corps. Dawson remained a career soldier for the rest of his working life, serving in India and, during the Second World War, in the United States. He retired with the rank of Colonel to Eastbourne in the south of England where he died in February, 1967. Cremated, he has no grave marker.

Second cousins, if not brothers, in arms, Pollock and Dawson brought distinction both upon themselves and also their home county. But what manner of men were they? By their apparently calm response to their enthusiastic receptions, they seem to have been very modest with a keen sense of what was right. Indeed Pollock, interviewed in 1952, declared, "I thought it my duty to volunteer and try to stop the progress of the Germans".

Also they both appear to have been conservative by nature, the evidence for this being the patriotic nature of their public pronouncements coupled with their choice of postwar careers.

Modest they may have been but they were also quietly proud of their wartime achievements. They regularly attended those most exclusive of parties, the commemorative VC celebrations, especially the 1956 Centenary Review in Hyde Park, an occasion they shared with a very different kind of hero, "Hoodoo" Kinross, the VC holder who also had family connections with Clackmannanshire (see Chapter 5). Perhaps these occasions, where they rubbed shoulders with fellow warriors, were where they were most at home, mingling with other ordinary men who knew what it was like to do something extraordinary.

The final Clackmannanshire man so far to receive the Victoria Cross is, at first glance anyway, a more colourful character than our previous recipients. Meet John Crawford Buchan, journalist, mountaineer, linguist, musician and last, but most certainly not least, ventriloquist.

John Crawford Buchan was born in King Street, Alloa, on October 10, 1892, the third son of David Buchan, the owner and editor of the local paper, *The Alloa Advertiser*, and his wife, Margaret. As the family grew in number to four boys and two girls, they moved to more spacious quarters at 5 Kellie Place.

Like James Lennox Dawson, Buchan was educated at Alloa Academy, a school with a proud list of former pupils who have distinguished themselves on the field of battle and elsewhere. After leaving school in 1910, John was apprenticed to Charles Thomson, the Town Clerk, with a view to entering the legal profession. However the scent of printing ink proved too strong to resist and he became a reporter on his father's paper in 1912. He loved writing and provided articles on climbing and the outdoors to the national daily, *The Scotsman*, in addition to his everyday work at the *Advertiser*. A keen sportsman, he played rugby and even caused a minor sensation by skiing in the nearby Ochil Hills. During his holidays he worked at the Scottish YMCA Summer Camp which suggests that he belonged to that band of "muscular Christians", so many of whom went on to become junior officers and, too often, casualties.

While at school, John had discovered that he had a gift for languages and so, taking this together with his keen interest in outdoor pursuits, it's not so surprising that he was in Switzerland in the fateful summer of 1914. Resident in the Alpine resort of Leysin, he found himself cut off from home when war broke out. Fortunately he was able to earn a crust as an interpreter/clerk in a local hotel where he remained for a year until he received the papers necessary for him to journey home via France.

Immediately upon reaching London he volunteered for the Army and was assigned after basic training to the Royal Army Medical Corps to prepare hospitals to receive the expected flood of wounded. After two months of this work, his abilities were presumably recognised and he was commissioned with the rank of 2nd Lieutenant in the 7th Battalion of the Argyll & Sutherland Highlanders which drew most of its recruits from his home county of Clackmannanshire. By September, 1917, he was ready and embarked for France on what would unfortunately prove to be a one-way ticket.

On March 21, 1918, John Crawford Buchan found himself on the outskirts of the village of Marteville on the Upper Somme where he and his men were about to bear the brunt of the "Kaiserschlacht". Also known as Operation Michael or the Spring Offensive, this "Kaiser's Battle" was the savage blitzkrieg launched by the Germans in a last desperate attempt to smash the Allies before the Americans arrived in force. Lieutenant Buchan, all of 25 years of age, was about to have his name entered in the book of heroes.

The *London Gazette* of May 21, 1918, provides us with a very full account of the last hours of this young man who once had a bright future ahead of him:

"For most conspicuous bravery and devotion to duty. When fighting with his platoon in the forward position of the battle zone, 2nd Lieutenant Buchan, although wounded early in the day, insisted on remaining with his men and continually visited all his posts, encouraging and cheering his men in spite of most severe shell fire from which his platoon was suffering heavy casualties. Later, when the enemy were creeping closer and heavy machine-gun fire was raking his position, 2nd Lieutenant Buchan, with utter disregard of his personal safety, continued to visit his posts. Eventually, when he saw the enemy had practically surrounded his command, he collected his platoon and prepared to fight his way back to the supporting line.

At this point, the enemy, who had crept round his right flank, rushed towards him, shouting out, 'Surrender!'.

'To hell with surrender!' he replied and, shooting the foremost of the enemy, he finally repelled this advance with his platoon. He then fought his way back to the supporting line of the forward position where he held out until dusk. At dusk he fell back as ordered but, in spite of his injuries, again refused to go to the aid post, saying his place was with his men. Owing to the unexpected withdrawal of troops on the left flank it was impossible to send orders to 2nd Lieutenant Buchan to withdraw as he was already cut off and he was last seen holding out against overwhelming odds.

The gallantry, self-sacrifice and utter disregard of personal safety displayed by this officer during these two days of most severe fighting is in keeping with the highest traditions of the British Army."

An even greater accolade came from one of his men: "He never asked us to do what he would not do himself".

So ended the short military career and life of John Crawford Buchan, sportsman, writer, scholar and, apparently, a genuinely good fellow. Oh! I almost forgot – he was locally also much in demand as a ventriloquist. Whether his two dummies, Johnny and Sammy, went with him to the Western Front we shall never know. Perhaps they are still somewhere in a suitcase waiting for another friendly hand to bring them to life. Unfortunately, no hand, friendly or otherwise, could do anything for young John. He died of his wounds in a German field hospital on either the 21st or 22nd March, 1918.

The editor's boy was only one among thousands of British troops who perished in that springtime long ago. The Kaiserschlacht very nearly succeeded but, fortunately, it failed, for a variety of reasons, not the least of which were the last ditch stands made by such soldiers as John Crawford Buchan, VC. He now rests in the cemetery at Roisel, not far from Marteville, along with another 734 British and Commonwealth dead and 514 Germans, united forever by their common destiny.

The Buchan family did not have a good war. In fact, they had an awful one. David Buchan, an apparently brilliant scholar at St Andrews University, was killed on April 9, 1917, while serving with the Gordon Highlanders. Francis Buchan died of wounds in August, 1918. Norman Buchan survived. Extremely short-sighted, he remained with his father at the *Advertiser*. No "My Boy Jack" scenario there, thankfully. Robert Buchan, another brilliant scholar, reputedly fluent in seven languages, survived the War and had a very distinguished career in the Diplomatic Service. He died in harness as Consul General in Amsterdam in 1938 and so he didn't have much of an innings either. The elder sister, Meg, looked after the family after her mother died and did Red Cross work locally during the War. The fates weren't going

to allow her to escape from their malignant grip, however; her fiancée drowned in the bath after inhaling toxic fumes at work. Jessie also helped at home and did some nursing. She married a Fred Proudfoot after the War with whom, let's hope, she found some happiness. The Buchans, a remarkably talented family, were an unbelievably tragic one as well. It was almost preordained that John's VC would be a posthumous one.

Lest we forget, we began this narrative with the story of John McDermond and it is to him that we return for this last reflection. Totally unknown in his home county and lying in an unmarked plot in Paisley, John McDermond, VC, could well stand for all those men, medal winners and otherwise, who, duty done, have been consigned to the darkness as the years slip away.

* * *

Postscript

For those wishing to visit the actual Victoria Crosses won by the four Wee County heroes and other commemorative sites, here are the details.

- John McDermond: Location unknown. However the painting of his VC action can be viewed at the Queen's Lancashire Regimental Museum in Preston.
- James Dalglish Pollock: The Highlanders Museum at Fort George, near Inverness.
- James Lennox Dawson: The Hunterian Museum, the University of Glasgow.
- John Crawford Buchan: Stirling Castle. There is also an artist's impression of his VC action in Alloa Town Hall.

This sepia tone drawing was executed by the renowned war artist, Fortunata Matania, for *Sphere* magazine in 1918. The original was purchased by Alloa Town Council and

"To Hell with Surrender!"

displayed in the Public Library. It then hung in Alloa Academy for a number of years before ending up in Alloa Town Hall.

Pollock and Dawson are also commemorated in their home town of Tillicoultry on memorial plaques located in a prominent position on the High Street. These were unveiled in 2015 on the 100th anniversary of the Battle of Loos.

CHAPTER 13

YPRES: REFLECTIONS AND MEMORIES

O VER the years the Flemish town of Ypres has come to mean more to me than ever I thought possible. Of course I was aware of its existence as I grew up. What British boy of my generation had not heard at some time or other of "Wipers" from the old soldiers who had fought there during the Great War though I suspect that few of them had any desire to return to the ruined town round which so many of their pals had died. Yet to me and those thousands of battlefield tourists who flock there every year, the town is once again a fair city where to sit on a café terrace on the main square with the Cloth Hall and Cathedral in the background is one of life's finer moments. But there's much more to Ypres than a chance to enjoy café society and people watching.

I'm going to take you on a tour which, though far from comprehensive, might help to explain why the town keeps drawing me back.

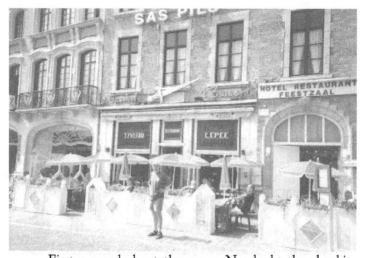

First a word about the name. No doubt the clued-in among you will have spotted that I've used the French spelling, "Ypres", for the town, whereas on all contemporary maps and motorway signs the Flemish version, "Ieper", is employed. However I've decided to go with "Ypres" at the risk of offending my Flemish friends, because everything in this chapter will have a connection to the First or Second World War when the town was known as "Ypres". Flemish, a variant of Dutch, is now the official language of Flanders, that area of northern Belgium where Ypres lies. Hence the change today from 'Ypres' to 'Ieper'. This linguistic division between the Flemish speaking northerners and the French speaking inhabitants (Walloons) of the southern half of Belgium, Wallonia, has bitter roots planted deep in the past. The divide goes far beyond language, of course, but it would be foolhardy of me to attempt to explain its origins here. Let's just acknowledge that it's always there, a fact of everyday life cropping up, often unexpectedly, in ways that might appear trivial to outsiders but which are deadly serious to those involved.

Today, Ypres is a prosperous town about an hour's drive from the Channel ports. Relying on tourism and some industry it supports a population of 35,000 if you include the surrounding villages. Surprisingly this is 5000 short of the figure in the Middle Ages when its great prosperity was based on the wool trade with England. Links established then were forever strengthened during the Great War, the commemoration of which now provides a very substantial chunk of the town's income. You only have to stand on the Grote Markt (market square) and look around at the cafes and chocolate shops to see the proof of that. Commerce will have to wait, however. St Martin's Cathedral is calling.

Now you may have deduced from previous chapters that I'm not what could be described as in any way religious. Yet I like churches and respect the part they've played in their communities over the centuries. And there's a lot about St Martin's to like, its dim vastness to start with and the many

memorials, plaques, tableaux and tombs which miraculously survived the battering the old girl took during the War.

Usually I save St Martin's for the last morning of my visit when I'm spending time prior to heading off to Zeebrugge and the boat for home. Inevitably I end up by reading this poem which you'll find tucked away on a side wall.

YPRES CATHEDRAL
1930

The organ throbs, its echoes die away,
A shaft of light, rose-tinted makes a track
That dwells upon an altar breathing peace.
I sit, and in my reverie look back...
The walls dissolve, the moonlight filters through,
The stars above shine out in fitful sky,
The altar yawns, the graves again gape wide,
And ghostly voices breathe a murmured sigh.
As in a dream I hear again the sound
Of transport rattle over cobbled street
 The distant drum that tells of lurking death,
And the beating pulse of countless marching feet.
A nearby gun booms out its warning note,
I hear the venomed answer whining by,
The earth again is shattered and I hear
A whinny of alarm, and then a cry...
The organ swells, the darkness fades away,
I struggle to the present from the past.
The hum of ghostly voices intertwines
With cadences that breathe of peace at last.

But still there lingers in this town of Dreams
Where every stone is sanctified by dead
A breath of English lanes and hopes of youth.
I sigh and then in silence hang my head.

(Found among the papers of Brigadier
General H.M. Hordern, OBE, MC,
and considered written by him)

The only information I've been able to dig up about the poet is that he was in the Royal Garrison Artillery and went to Eton, which brings us nicely to our next port of call, St George's Memorial Church.

This very English church lies just across A. Vandepeereboomplein (the Flemish must have a sense of humour) from the Cathedral. What's the connection with Eton? Round the back of the church, is the British School

which was built in the 1920s with funds raised by Old Etonians to commemorate those of their fellows who fell at Ypres. The main impetus behind the fund-raising was provided by the then-Provost (headmaster) of Eton, M.R. James. For those of you who like frightening yourself half to death, he is indeed *that* M.R. James, Montague Rhodes James, author of perhaps the finest tales of the supernatural ever to be committed to paper. Anyway, he raised the necessary cash and the School was opened in 1927. The pupils were almost exclusively the children of the gardeners of the Imperial War Graves Commission, those British ex-servicemen who had stayed behind to care for the war cemeteries that were being established. Most of these gardeners married local girls and so the pupils had the benefit of a bi-lingual upbringing at home. The education they received at the School, however, was firmly based on the English language and loyalty to the British Empire. The School functioned very successfully during the interwar years, right up until the German blitzkrieg of 1940 when pupils, parents and staff dispersed, most to safety in Britain though some remained and were interned. A minority, remarkably, managed to stay on in Ypres where several were involved in clandestine operations.

For an excellent account of the School before and during World War II, I can thoroughly recommend *The Children Who Fought Hitler* by Sue Elliott and James Fox, while Dr Gillian Hawke's monograph, *Greater Love Hath No Man: St George's Memorial Church, Ypres*, deals with the history of the Church itself.

By the time peace was restored in 1945, the British presence in Ypres was greatly diminished and the School never reopened. Instead the building assumed a dual function as St George's Church Hall and the Royal British Legion Club where the CWGC gardeners and locals would socialise at weekends. One of those

locals was Ivan Sinnaeve. This was his given name but he was much better known as Shrapnel Charlie.

A carpenter by trade, Charlie injured his back so severely at work in 1991 that he had to use a wheelchair thereafter to negotiate all but the shortest distances. However his life was to change for the better four years later when, after seeing some toy soldiers in a shop, he decided, "I can do that!" and indeed he could. Over the next seventeen years he made thousands of them using shrapnel from the former battlefields. Melting the once lethal balls and shards of metal in the furnace in his home workshop, Charlie cast and painted exquisite miniatures which he sold for charity. Charlie's production line brought him no riches but it did earn him the respect of his many friends from all over the globe.

The first time I met Charlie was at Ulster Tower on the Somme where he was on a shrapnel gathering expedition. On that occasion, after hearing my Scots accent, he presented me with a little Highlander which I treasure still. The only other time I saw him was at Track "X" Cemetery near Ypres when he was present at the interment of the remains of some British soldiers which had been uncovered during an archaeological dig.

He was there, as he was at all such ceremonial occasions, to pay his respects, formally dressed but with his trademark Glengarry perched jauntily on his head.

Charlie's ultimate goal was to produce as many of his meticulously crafted soldiers as there are names on the Memorial to the Missing at the Menin Gate in Ypres. Unfortunately he never realised his dream. Charlie died in March, 2012, at just 59 years of age. Gone he might be, but he's fondly remembered by all those who were privileged to know him. Now I'll never be able to buy him that beer...

Talking of which – beer, I mean – I'd like to take you for a glass at the Shell Hole. I'd like to, but I can't. Like Charlie it's gone forever but, again like Charlie, it's not forgotten.

What a place it was! Run by John and Christine, it was a combination of bed and breakfast hotel, book and militaria shop and a bar – or should that be *the* bar! Tucked away up D'Hondstraat about 200 metres from the Grote Markt, the Shell Hole nonetheless managed to attract a wide variety of customers to the shop by day and the bar at night. Battlefield tourists, local politicians and worthies and CWGC gardeners mixed, chatted and generally learned from each other. Soldiers past and present came to confer with John, a Falklands veteran himself. Sometimes, during the week, it could be quiet but, come the weekend, it was bursting with life. Outside it might be cold and rainy and the streets deserted but in the bar at the Shell Hole there would be warmth, light, people and, above all, laughter. Then John and Christine retired to Provence and the party was over.

John and Christine, The Shell Hole

The building still is there, now the very pleasant Hotel Ambrosia, but the Shell Hole has gone and with it a major part of my life in Ypres. Sometimes I walk past the hotel at night and stop momentarily just in case ghosts do exist. Those were the days, my friend, and I was lucky to share in them. I hoped they'd never end but, like everything in life, they did...

Much of what I know about Ypres, past and present, I learned in the bar at the Shell Hole. There you could ask about most things quite freely but one subject had to be very carefully negotiated: the question of collaboration and resistance during World War II.

I first became aware of resistance activity in the Ypres area when I came across an information board by the railway next to the Hill 60

car park. It tells the sad tale of two local lads who were shot by the Germans in 1944 for alleged sabotage. It started me thinking – and cautiously enquiring.

Apparently there was both resistance and collaboration round about Ypres. As might be expected, the majority of citizens, though deeply resenting the German presence, just tried to keep a low profile and got on with the business of day-to-day survival. But there was also resistance here. The Hotel Regina on the corner of the Grote Markt and Rijselsestraat (Lille Street) was a station on the Comet Line, an escape route to neutral Spain for Allied airmen who'd been shot down on raids over the Continent. In addition, the execution of the two boys at Hill 60 suggests that acts of sabotage occurred locally.

On the other hand both Flanders and Wallonia contributed Waffen SS Divisions to the German Army to back up its beleaguered forces on the Eastern Front. For the Germans it was relatively easy to get support for their recruitment campaign in both regions by playing on the fear of

Commemorative stone to members of the Resistance from the Second World War

On 2nd September 1944 Pierre Marchant and Lucien Ollivier, two Frenchmen, members of the Resistance, were on a lorry loaded with munitions near the station of their hometown La Madeleine, close to Lille (Fr).

A German train arrived in the station and a group of S.S. circled immediately the lorry. The driver and his escort were captured and taken on the train to Belgium. This train, packed with soldiers and firearms, stopped at the border between Zillebeke and Hollebeke. As usual, it must wait an extra reinforcement from a locomotive coming from Ypres.

What happened exactly at this place, was not clearly established.

Have they tried to escape from the train ?

Have they received the order, from the Germans, to jump out the train ?

Residents have heard gunshots that evening.

On one of the verges of the railway, two hundred meters from here, the inanimate bodies of this two young people were found.

A burial place, in the Zillebeke's village, temporarily accommodated them. Later, their bodies were transported to their residence's place where each received a final burial place.

Bolshevism among devout Catholics. In Flanders, as an extra sweetener, the Germans implied that there would be more regional autonomy for the Flemings.

The Shell Hole had its part to play in this. "Old Bill" used to come in during the day for a cup of coffee and a chat. Nothing unusual in that, you might say, except for the fact that he always wore his Waffen SS cap – and carpet slippers.

Yes, he had been a member of the Flemish Legion, for which he showed no remorse or regret. As he saw it, he had been fighting for Catholicism against the Red Menace. Occasionally at night another link to wartime Ypres would appear for a quiet drink. Georges, who had been in the Resistance, was a Socialist who had also fought for what he believed in. He divulged very little of his past except to say that for the last six months of the occupation he had been, often literally, in the underground movement hiding out in cellars and on farms. He was a nice old man but, there again, so was Bill. Both are dead now but their legacy remains.

At the end of the Occupation, of course, the reckoning had to come. Those convicted of closely collaborating with the Germans faced imprisonment or the firing squad. Others suspected of minor acts of collaboration faced recrimination, acts of vengeance and the general settling of old scores all of

Georges of the Resistance (right), in the Shell Hole with my great friend, the late Jimmy Calder

which left a bitter legacy. Apparently there are still a few families in the Ypres area who can't forget what their parents or grandparents did during World War II. Like latter day Montagues and Capulets, they keep to themselves, meeting from time to time in the backrooms of chosen cafés where they can celebrate or attempt to justify their particular pasts. Lest you think I exaggerate, let me quote from *Flanders Today* of May 25, 2011:

> "The question of Belgium's wartime record of collaboration is still a thorny issue and one that divides Flanders and Wallonia to

this day. Both sides had collaborationists, from the Rexist Party in Wallonia to the Flemish National Union (VNV), plus the Flemish and Wallon Legions, both divisions of the Waffen SS. Part of that collaboration took the form of helping to deport some 25,000 Belgian Jews to Auschwitz. About 1,200 survived. After the War, 400,000 Belgians were investigated as suspected collaborators, with 56,000 convicted. The death penalty was exercised in 242 cases. By 1950, only about 2,500 were still in prison; the others had either served their time or had been pardoned."

This was in response to the furore that arose in the wake of an unguarded remark by Belgium's Federal Minister of Justice who had proposed a debate on an amnesty for wartime collaborators, saying that it was "time to forget the past". Despite an attempt to backtrack by the minister, "The statement continues to cause anger, as does the question of amnesty for collaborators".

As the 21st century rolls on, perhaps these bitter divisions will simply wither away. But who can tell? Especially in Ypres, a town built on remembrance. Nowhere can this be more powerfully felt than at the massive Memorial to the Missing at the Menin Gate.

During the First World War, the Menin Gate was on the main road to and from the front line. Virtually every British or Commonwealth soldier sent to fight around Ypres passed through the Gate, many, of course, never to return. By the Armistice in 1918 it had become almost a legend among the troops. Where better then to erect the major shrine of remembrance in the Ypres Salient?

Various plans had been put forward for the building of a memorial in the town. Winston Churchill proposed that the British Government should purchase all of the ruins of Ypres and let the poppies take over. However the doughty citizens of Ypres, who had begun to trickle back almost as soon as the last shell had been fired, had other ideas. Various other schemes were floated until, in the end, the Belgian Government, thoroughly alarmed by some of the proposals, offered the Menin Gate site to the British and construction began. After many technical difficulties had been overcome, Sir Reginald Blomfield's masterpiece, his monument to those who went missing in the mud and madness that was Wipers, was finally unveiled on 24 July, 1927.

The Menin Gate today

The Menin Gate in the 1930s

Surprisingly perhaps, unlike most memorials the Menin Gate does not exist in an atmosphere of sombre solemnity. It can do so as the occasion requires, but usually the Gate is full of life. Cars and cyclists pass through going about their daily business. The voices of schoolchildren echo cheerfully while quieter, older visitors try to make sense of the seemingly endless lists of nearly 59,000 names on the white panels of Portland stone. But in the evening, everything changes for a short while. At precisely 8.00 pm, a policeman closes the road to traffic and the buglers of the Ypres Fire Brigade play the Last Post – every night, regardless of the weather, even on Christmas Day. Maybe that should read "especially on Christmas Day". So it has gone on ever since the unveiling in 1927, except for the years of German occupation when the ceremony was "*verboten*". The very day the Germans were driven out of town by the Poles in 1944 the buglers were back to fill the arches with their glorious sound. One of them was a young Antoon Verschoot. He died in February, 2017, aged 91, having been actively involved at "the Gate" until very shortly before his death – a quite remarkable man.

When I first went to the ceremony in 1981 there were very few people in attendance. The day of Ypres as a major tourist centre had not yet arrived. Today it's a different story. To get a decent view of the proceedings you have to arrive about forty five minutes beforehand or else be seven feet tall. OK for Dutch people but not for a wee Scotsman. Often the ceremony is a major production with marching bands, pipers and wreath laying, all magnificently organised by the Last

Last Post at the Menin Gate:
Antoon Verschoot is shown in the middle

Post Committee. Got to keep up with the times, I suppose, but, do you know, I think I preferred the old days when it was just a few pilgrims, the buglers, the echoes and that old man with his dog.

Despite the memorial being dismissed, not unexpectedly, in 1928 by Siegfried Sassoon as a "sepulchre of crime" in his poem 'On Passing the New Menin Gate', with the greatest of respect, I think he got it wrong for once. Maybe the last words on the subject, in this context at least, should be left to Lord Plumer of Messines, good old Daddy Plumer, the soldiers' soldier. At the Unveiling Ceremony, he declared:

> "One of the most tragic features of the Great War was the number of casualties reported as missing... therefore it was resolved that here at Ypres... there should be erected a memorial worthy of them which should give expression to the nation's gratitude... A memorial has been erected which fulfils this objective and now it can be said of each one, He is not missing; he is here!"

That's my snapshot of Ypres then. A place equally of infinite good cheer and great solemnity. A town where you can wander through the shadows of the past or sit in the sunlight sipping a beer.

Ypres lives. After all, isn't that what all those "nameless names" and their comrades fought and died for?

CHAPTER 14

CEMETERIES, HEROES
AND A BIG MONKEY

N O ONE who has visited the Western Front can fail to have been impressed by the cemeteries so beautifully maintained by the Commonwealth War Graves Commission (CWGC). Havens of peace and tranquillity, they are also very interesting places and once past the initial and inevitable flood of emotion that can often

The Ramparts Cemetery, Ypres

overwhelm the visitor then curiosity begins to take over. And for the curious there's much to be learned – or puzzled over. For example, how about this inscription on a stone in Aubigny-en-Artois Communal Extension Cemetery near Arras?

IT'S DARK DOWN HERE

What do you make of that then? Or this one in Abeele Aerodrome Cemetery near Poperinghe in Belgium from the headstone of Private Fern of the West Yorkshire Regiment killed in July, 1918, aged nineteen:

OLD PAL WHY DON'T YOU ANSWER ME

Then there's the "Aristocrats' Cemetery" in Zillebeke churchyard, near Ypres, where the gravestone of Lieutenant Colonel Gordon Chesney Wilson bears words culled from a verse reaching back to the Middle Ages:

LIFE IS A CITY OF CROOKED STREETS DEATH THE MARKET PLACE WHERE ALL MEN MEET

If you weren't thinking of your own mortality when you came in, you certainly will be on the way out.

Not far from Zillebeke in the vast Lijssenthoek Cemetery is the grave of Staff Nurse Nellie Spindler from Wakefield, killed by a shell while on duty near the front line in August 1917, aged 26. She remains now and forever more:

A NOBLE TYPE OF GOOD HEROIC WOMANHOOD

Though death, as was pointed out in Zillebeke Churchyard, is the great leveller, there are inevitably some casualties of the War who are remembered more than others, achieving in death a kind of celebrity status. Such a one is the American, Alan Seeger.

Born into a wealthy New York family, Alan led a life of privilege as a young man – Harvard University and then on to Gay Paree with all that entailed. However the good times came to an abrupt end on, ironically, United States Independence Day, 1916, when he was killed in action at Belloy-en-Santerre near Amiens while serving in the ranks of the French Foreign Legion. His best known poem,

"Rendezvous", proved to be an eerie and absolutely accurate forecast of his own death. It begins:

"I have a rendezvous with death/At some disputed barricade..."

Alan kept his rendezvous, but he's not forgotten in Belloy. The church bells, which were given to the village by his

parents, are rung every Sunday and on the wall of the Mairie there's a floral plaque in his memory.

The main reason Alan Seeger interests me, apart from his poetry, is that he was the uncle of one of my heroes, the American folk singer Pete Seeger, political activist and general thorn in the flesh of those who perpetrate injustice upon others. Probably his best known song is the civil rights anthem "We Shall Overcome", but he's had many other notable successes including "Where Have All The Flowers Gone?" A more appropriate song, with its strong anti-war sentiments, to carry in your mental kitbag while visiting the battlefields would be hard to find. So, never one to shy away from outrageously sentimental gestures, I whistled it as I strolled round Belloy. As I approached the end of my rendition, I noticed the teacher in the village school looking at

me from her classroom window. I wonder if she made any connection or just saw a crazy old coot making an annoying noise?

One last thing before we leave Alan Seeger. I think it's worth a mention that "Rendezvous" was the favourite poem of President Kennedy.

These young people, along with

millions more, were cherished by those they left behind to grieve. Nowhere is this sense of loss better expressed than in the German cemetery at Vladslo, near Diksmuide in Belgium. There the mass grave where Peter Kollwitz lies is overlooked by two massive statues, known as "The Grieving Parents", created by his mother, Kathe. Peter's death in the ranks of the student battalions near Ypres in October, 1914, had devastated his mother to such an extent that her deep sorrow could only be assuaged by total immersion in her work. A committed pacifist and socialist, Kathe's art later came to be hated by the Nazis. Nevertheless her masterpiece survived and remains today, a sombre reminder of the grief suffered by all parents, regardless of nationality, who had lost children.

Before we leave the subject of the cemeteries, what of the men and women who maintain these "silent cities"? Each time I stayed at the Shell Hole in Ypres I would meet CWGC gardeners, all of whom had a tale to tell – nothing sensational, just reflections on their everyday work or on characters, living

and dead, whom they had come across. One very old man had been a member of the mobile squads during the interwar years and after World War Two. These units would set up camp at a designated location on Monday morning and work through the week recovering bodies from small remote graveyards and reinterring them in the larger concentration cemeteries where maintenance would be much easier. This particular gardener, the son of a British soldier who had remained in Flanders after the Great War to work for the Imperial War Graves Commission as the CWGC was then known, had been "the lad" or general go-fer on his squad. The most important of his tasks, he told me, was to go to any nearby village shop to fetch the week's groceries, among which would often be a bottle of whisky. Considered by some gaffers to be an absolute necessity, Scotland's finest was used not only to ward off the cold, but also to make the handling of the decaying corpses which were being transferred to their final resting place a little more bearable.

Some of my acquaintances who have never been to the Western Front are quite understandably puzzled by my cemetery visits, a question I touched upon in Chapter 2. I think I'll leave it to Henry Williamson, author of the much loved *Tarka the Otter* and a veteran of the Great War, to explain in this extract from *The Wet Flanders Plain*:

> "...The dead who died upon these battlefields in such agony as no one who was not there can ever know, lie in French cemeteries, German cemeteries, British and Commonwealth cemeteries, at peace. Which means that we the living who visit them find

peace there: and wholeness, which may be
the same thing as holiness."

And why do I, an irreligious person, lay my hand
sometimes on an individual headstone? Once again I'll go to
an outside source for an answer, this time Diana Gurney in
her poem 'The Fallen':

"We do not know, perhaps a breath
Of our remembering may come
To them at last where they are sleeping."

All of this, the cemeteries and the emotions they evoke,
would not be possible had it not been for the vision of one
remarkable man, Fabian Ware, whose legacy is defined thus
by David Crane in *Empires of the Dead*:

"...no one in the history of warfare had
transferred the horrors and suffering of a
battlefield into oases of peace like Ware."

Anyone who visits the battlefields is never far away
from a cemetery, either literally or afterwards in their
thoughts. One graveyard in particular remains indelibly
imprinted on the memory of those who visit it and all because
of one of its occupants. In Brandhoek Number 3 which lies
between Ypres and Poperinghe, you will find the most visited
individual grave on the Western Front, that of Captain Noel
Chavasse, MC, VC and Bar.

Noel Chavasse was born in 1884 in Oxford where his father was an Anglican clergyman. In 1900 the family moved to Liverpool when the Reverend Chavasse was appointed Bishop of that city. By 1904 Noel had returned to Oxford to enter Trinity College, graduating in 1907 with First Class Honours in Medicine. During his time in the city of dreaming spires and during his vacation time back in Liverpool, as was expected of one of his background, he did good work with poor boys in church missions and at summer camps. Remarkably, given his academic and charitable workload, he also found time to excel at sports, particularly rugby and running. In fact both he and his twin brother, Christopher, participated in the 400 metres in the 1908 Olympic Games in London. Even though both were eliminated from the competition when they came second and third respectively in their heat, it still remains a remarkable achievement. By the time the War broke out in 1914, Chavasse was not only a fully qualified and experienced surgeon but he had also been appointed as a surgeon lieutenant in the Territorial Army to the 10th Battalion of the King's Liverpool Regiment, better known as the Liverpool Scottish.

So that was the pre-war life of Noel Chavasse, a life that was in many ways typical of so many young men of his class – diligent and successful study, voluntary work with the less fortunate members of society, a work ethic based on a strong belief in the Christian faith and a '*mens sana in corpore sano*' approach to leisure activity, all of which left little or no time for frivolous pursuits. And so late in 1914, Noel along with all the rest of his soldier brethren, Christian and otherwise, went marching unto war.

Having been used to a regime of public service, self-discipline and sacrifice, Chavasse was well equipped to deal with the rigours of military life. From 1915 to 1917 he compiled a remarkable record of decorations for gallantry. First came the Military Cross won at Hooge near Ypres in June 1915, a "Mentioned in Despatches" in November 1915, the Victoria Cross on August 9, 1916 at Guillemont on the Somme and then finally and tragically, another Victoria Cross for his actions over the period July 31 to August 2, 1917, at Wieltje, once again near Ypres. All of these awards were for bringing in and tending the wounded while under intense enemy fire. Unlike most other recipients of the VC, Chavasse's awards were for saving life, not taking it.

His death had a sort of inevitability about it. Continually going out into No Man's Land to succour the wounded and working at advanced dressing stations in the front line, it was only a matter of time before his luck, if you can call it that, ran out. He could perhaps have survived a while longer if he had agreed to have his severe wounds attended to at Wieltje but that wasn't the Chavasse style. Ignoring the pain he went on – and on – bringing in the wounded and tending to their injuries unflinchingly until he had no more left to give. He died of his wounds and general loss of blood at a dressing station at Brandhoek near to where he lies today.

En route he had been given first aid by Lieutenant Colonel Arthur Martin-Leake, which was quite a coincidence as Martin-Leake was also a double VC having won his first award in 1902 during the Boer War. And here he was in the thick of the conflict, trying to save the life of the man who would soon join him in the ranks of the bravest of the brave. Interestingly the coincidence does not stop there. The only other double VC is Captain Charles Upham from New Zealand who won his medals in Crete and at El Alamein during the Second World War. He was related to Noel Chavasse by marriage. There are still today only three double VCs and the common link is Noel Chavasse.

For a much more detailed and rounded picture of the man, I encourage you to read Ann Clayton's probably definitive biography, *Chavasse: Double VC.* She shows him

as the remarkable man he was – compassionate, honest, humorous in a dry way, intolerant of humbug and unafraid to criticise any failings which he perceived in staff officers, fellow medical officers and padres, in fact anyone who was not one hundred per cent behind the common soldier.

Noel Chavasse was one of the bravest

men who has ever lived. He walked through the Valley of Death yet seemed, truly, to fear none ill and remains to this day the very epitome of a true Christian.

Finally I'd like to introduce you to two characters for whom I have the warmest affection, one a glorious maverick and the other – well, you'll see.

First up is the Reverend Geoffrey Anketell Studdert Kennedy, MC, who revelled in the nickname "Woodbine Willie".

Pre-war he was a parish priest in Worcester where he devoted himself tirelessly to helping the poor. Always up for a fight, sometimes literally in the boxing ring, he campaigned constantly against social injustice. When war came he joined up as a chaplain but was not one of those who spent most of

their time well away from the danger zone. "Willie" cheered up the front line troops by sharing not only their dangers but also his seemingly inexhaustible supply of 'Woodbine' cigarettes and talking to them in words they could understand. He, like Chavasse, spent much time in No Man's Land looking for wounded men, actions for which he was awarded the Military Cross. Long after the

War, "Woodbine Willie" was still fighting, as he had done all his adult life, for a better deal for the poor. In 1929, worn out by self-sacrifice, hard work and Woodbines, the Reverend Kennedy, MC, drew his final breath. But he didn't go to his final resting place alone. Hundreds turned out for his funeral including many of those soldiers for whom he'd done so much in both peace and war. There, at the graveside in Worcester, they threw their Woodbines on to the coffin to accompany their padre on his way. They'd come to give their champion – "Woodbine Willie", chaplain, poet, fighter and smoker – the best send-off they could think of, and they succeeded.

Now last but by no means least we come to that "other" whom I mentioned above; Jackie, the Soldier Baboon. Albert Marr found the infant Jackie on his family's farm near Pretoria in South Africa and "adopted" him. As he grew to adulthood Jackie became so humanised that, when Albert signed on with the 3rd South African Infantry Regiment in August, 1915, he requested permission for Jackie to accompany him. Because of his good behaviour and very impressive stature, Jackie was taken on as the regimental mascot and was kitted out with his own uniform, pay book and rations.

Although baboons can be very aggressive and dangerous, Jackie never once blotted his copy book and became a great favourite, learning to salute correctly and even lighting the soldiers' cigarettes. In July, 1916, Jackie and Albert found themselves at the dreadful Battle of Delville Wood on the Somme. When Albert was wounded, Jackie remained with him,

JACKIE   Mascot of the 3RD 5TH AFRICAN INF.

licking his wound until the medics could get to him. Largely due to Jackie's ministrations, Albert made a full recovery and the partners resumed their military careers. In April 1918 Albert was wounded again and this time Jackie was also hit by a shell splinter. Remarkably, the Soldier Baboon, at the insistence of the men, was given his place in the queue for the operating theatre where his right leg was amputated. Equally remarkably, Jackie made a full recovery at a base hospital where he was soon sitting up and saluting the doctors. For Jackie and Albert the war was over but they weren't cast to the side. Instead they were used as fund-raisers for the Red Cross in Britain where they raised thousands of pounds. The big attraction, of course, was Jackie, who sold kisses for five shillings or handshakes for two and sixpence. Discharged in Cape Town in April, 1919, with a Gold wound Stripe on the left sleeve of his uniform and three blue service chevrons on his right, Jackie returned to the farm with Albert. He died, tragically, in a fire on the farm in 1921, a terrible end for one who'd survived the hell of the trenches.

Of all the stories I've come across during my reading and travelling, I think that the story of Jackie must be the most remarkable – and heart-warming. And it's with Jackie and Albert that I shall now close my meanderings. It's been fantastic fun while it lasted and, who knows, we might run into each other in the future on some abandoned battlefield or by one of those monuments to courage.

PERSONAL ACKNOWLEDGEMENTS

I would like to express my deep gratitude to the two people – my wife, **Janie**, and my friend **Andrew Stewart** – who have been with me from the very beginning of this enterprise. Without their help and encouragement it would quite simply not have come to pass.

Equally I wish to express the huge debt I owe to **Tom and Julie Christie**, my publishers, who have worked tirelessly to bring my work to a wider audience.

CHAPTER 4:
THE MYSTERIOUS DEATH OF CAPTAIN JOHN LAUDER

The staffs of the Mitchell Library, Glasgow, and the University of Glasgow Library, especially Claire McKendrick, Chief Library Assistant with special responsibility for the Scottish Theatre Archive. These ladies and gentlemen are acknowledged in a great number of publications for their sterling work in helping both aspiring and established authors. As an "aspirant", let me add my gratitude to an already long list.

Rod McKenzie, Curator of the A&SH Regimental Museum at Stirling Castle. Rod has been a huge help, not only in providing invaluable documentary information but also in helping me gain some sort of perspective on the John Lauder controversy.

Archie Wilson at the A&SH Museum was also extremely helpful.

Maureen, Visitor Adviser at Dunoon Tourist Office. Thank you for your courtesy and information provided on the Lauders in Dunoon.

Bob Bain, Honorary Secretary of the Scottish Music Hall & Variety Theatre Society. Many thanks for your interest, advice and photographic material provided.

James Marturano of New York. James is widely acknowledged as one of the leading Lauder experts and he has been extremely generous in sharing with me information which was hitherto unknown. His website is a treasure trove of all things Harry Lauder. James can be contacted at: www.sirharrylauder.com

Jim Vallance, has, like James Marturano, a vast collection of Harry Lauder memorabilia. He is also a descendant of Nance, Harry Lauder's wife. His generosity, like that of James, in providing material and advice has been invaluable to this project. Jim can be contacted at: jimvallance.com

Richard Gardiner of Liverpool. Richard provided me with much food for thought and gave me sound advice on some military aspects of the John Lauder story about which I knew nothing.

CHAPTER 5:
"HOODOO" KINROSS, VC, THE PRIDE OF LOUGHEED

Stan Kinross of Tillicoultry, Scotland, a distant cousin of Cecil John Kinross, VC, is the man who initially, by pointing me in the right direction, kick-started this whole enterprise. Stan's "right direction" was to...

Alistair Kinross and the Kinross family whose information has been invaluable and provided the factual base for most of Chapter 5.

Denise (Losness) Bratland Sigalet of Lougheed, Alberta, has also been absolutely vital to my research. Her family, Losness, emigrated from Norway in 1910. Like the Kinrosses, they settled in the Lougheed area. Denise tirelessly answered my many questions and, as I was unable to go to Lougheed personally, provided me with those personal details which put flesh on the bare bones of history. She also read the first draft and by so doing has, like the Kinross family, prevented me making any major errors of judgement.

Denise's husband, **Morris Sigalet**, provided photos of Lougheed without which it would be difficult for non-natives to visualise what Cecil's adopted home town is like. He also tracked down the very revealing images of Cecil which I had never seen before.

Jim Wright and Tom Barton of Lougheed generously provided important information to earlier researchers which has been passed on to me by the Kinross family.

My friend, the late **Jimmy Calder**, a frequent visitor to Canada and a fine geographer, was able to clue me in to the topography and climate of the Lougheed area, information which, taken in conjunction with Morris' photos, gave me a good idea of the country Cecil called home.

Debra Dittrick of the *Edmonton Journal* gave me access to the excellent article written for the paper by Bob Gilmour in 1989 and a great deal of additional information.

David Haas, Curator of the Loyal Edmonton Regimental Museum and Editor of *The Fortyniner*, first gave me permission to use the wonderful "Lestock" badge and also made many very useful suggestions. This permission was extended in 2017 by **Captain Terry Allison, CD**, Executive Director of the Loyal Edmonton Military Museum.

Tony Druett, who continues to keep alive the memory of Cecil and many other old soldiers both through his work with the Canadian Government and in his spare time, keeps me updated on commemorative activities in the Edmonton area.

The late **Henry L. Kirby** of Preston, Lancashire, military historian and broadcaster, inspired me to pursue my research in addition to giving me, through his own publications on the Great War, excellent examples of both substance and presentation. He was also one of those special people whom it is always a joy to meet.

Amanda Mason of the Department of Documents at the Imperial War Museum, London, allowed me access to the

Canon Lummis File of VC Recipients and very kindly provided photocopies of relevant material from it.

Lawrence Farrow, policeman of Ieper/Ypres, Belgium, guided me to the right places in the Canadian National Archive online and also helped in many other ways, notably with the location today of Furst Farm near which "Hoodoo" Kinross won his VC.

Jennifer Kolthammer steered me towards "Hoodoo's" military records. She is the wife of Brian Kolthammer, Cecil's great-nephew.

John Woolsgrove and Christine DeDeyne, former owners of the late Shell Hole Hotel, Pub and Bookshop in Ypres, were an ongoing source of information and help. I've known them since 1999 and greatly appreciate their kindness and advice over the years. Christine gave me an understanding of the complexities of Flemish politics, past and present, while John's knowledge of the battlefields and the War in general is second to none. Without their friendship I would not have returned as often as I did to the battlefields and hence this book might never have been written.

Last but by no means least, **Cecil John Kinross, VC**, the man himself, who provided me with hours of entertainment and much food for thought. I hope I've done right by him.

CHAPTER 6:
A WALK ACROSS THE ANCRE

Alan Marquis of Guernsey gave me a huge amount of guidance and information on an ongoing basis, especially about Ulster Tower.

Teddy and Phoebe Colligan: Thanks for the cups of tea, the always warm welcome and the great job you did at Ulster Tower.

Peter Hart, author, lecturer and, I suspect, bon viveur, provided me, through his excellent book 'Somme Success' (see bibliography) and his lectures, with much to ponder, especially in the way that battle fatigue/PTS disorder was treated by the RFC in stark contrast to the attitude of the Army in relation to Dyett.

CHAPTER 7:
TOMMY ARMOUR, THE IRON MASTER

Neil and Robert Dixon made a huge contribution to this chapter, Neil by unearthing the details of the *Weekly Record* contempt case and Robert by his research for me at the National Archives at Kew where he accessed Tommy Armour's military record. Without their help this chapter would have been greatly diminished.

Fiona Hastie of the Scottish Golf Union very promptly and courteously cleared up a mistaken perception about Sandy Armour's golf record.

Major Colin Hepburn, Regimental Secretary of the Royal Tank Regiment, kindly granted permission for the use of the images of the badges of the Machine Gun Corps and the Tank Regiment.

Andrew Main did a fine job on the photos of the Carnoustie Links which are on my website.

Brian Morrison contributed excellent background information on Tommy Armour's origins.

The staff at Register House in Edinburgh helped me to access the Armour Family Records and so laid to rest some mistakes which have been repeated down the years.

Jock Armour, Tommy's grandson, and the Armour family in the USA have been of great assistance in supplying additional information and guidance.

CHAPTER 8:
AN AUTUMN INTERLUDE

Alan Marquis for a splendid day on the Somme.

CHAPTER 9:
THE SHORT BUT EVENTFUL LIFE OF ALBERT BALL, VC

The staff at the Nottingham Archives, especially Bev, were extremely helpful.

As will be quite obvious to the reader, I have leaned somewhat heavily upon the works of **Chaz Bowyer** and **Colin Pengelly**. However the sources from which I derived most insight into Albert Ball and aerial warfare in WWI, are the books written by the inimitable **Peter Hart**. Indeed my interest in Albert Ball can be traced back to an excellent lecture delivered by Peter to the Tayside Branch of the WFA in January, 2009.

CHAPTER 11:
ON THE WARPATH

I am deeply indebted to **Izola Mottershead**, Alex Decoteau's niece, without whose help this chapter would not have been possible.

CHAPTER 12:
WEE COUNTY HEROES: CLACKMANNAN-SHIRE'S FOUR VCs

Jane Davies at the Museum of the Queen's Lancashire Regiment at Preston for her great help in researching McDermond, VC.

Brian Morrison for his work on the 1901 and 1911 Censuses and general information regarding Alloa and its Academy in days gone by.

Iain "Scoop" Stewart for his help in locating VC graves and also the whereabouts of the actual medals.

CHAPTER 13:
YPRES: REFLECTIONS AND MEMORIES

Previously acknowledged more fully in Chapter 5, **John Woolsgrove and Christine DeDeyne,** former owners of the Shell Hole.

Bobby Ross, a regular visitor to the battlefields as a tour guide has kept me abreast of contemporary developments on the Salient. He has proved to be an invaluable asset as well as excellent company.

I obviously owe a large debt of gratitude to my sources on Ypres during WWII but, for obvious reasons, they will have to remain anonymous.

CHAPTER 14:
CEMETERIES, HEROES AND A BIG MONKEY

Ian Mason (Brummy) and Paul, CWGC gardeners and really nice guys who provided me with much information about the CWGC and its work. Brum has since moved on to work with the local authority in Menin, Belgium, but we remain in touch. Paul has been promoted and remains in the Ypres area. I wish I knew his second name!

BIBLIOGRAPHY

1. GUIDEBOOKS

(i) **Rose E.B. Coombs**, *Before Endeavours Fade* (After the Battle Publications, 2006 Edition).
This was the first of the "modern" guides to the Great War battlefields as they are today. It is regularly updated and is excellent.
(ii) **Tonie and Valmai Holt**, *Major & Mrs Holt's Battlefield Guide to the Somme* (Pen & Sword, 1996).
–, *Major & Mrs Holt's Battlefield Guide to the Ypres Salient* (Pen & Sword, 1997).
–, *Major & Mrs Holt's Battlefield Guide to the Western Front: North* (Pen & Sword, 2004).
–, *Major & Mrs Holt's Battlefield Guide to the Western Front: South* (Pen & Sword, 2005).
All four of the Holts' books are readily obtainable and I can't emphasise too strongly just how essential they are. I would guess that they're unsurpassable in their field.
I shall be referring to the five books above throughout this work and shall indicate their specific use as appropriate in the text rather than in the bibliography to each chapter.
(iii) **Lieut.-Col. T.A. Lowe**, *The Western Battlefields* (Gale & Polden, 1920).
(iv) **Michael Scott**, *The Ypres Salient: A Guide To The Cemeteries And Memorials Of The Salient* (Gliddon Books, 1992).

2. SPECIFIC BOOKS AND MAGAZINES

Chapter 2

John Buchan, *These For Remembrance* (Buchan & Enright Publishers, 1987).
Facsimile edition of volume originally printed privately in 1919.
Andrew Lownie, *John Buchan: The Presbyterian Cavalier*, (Constable, 1995).

Chapter 3

John Reed, *Operation Jericho: The Amiens Raid* (*After the Battle Magazine* # 2, 1980).

Chapter 4

David Clarke, *The Angel of Mons* (John Wiley & Sons Limited, 2005).
A very fine demonstration of the power of myth over truth and therefore extremely relevant to understanding the John Lauder conundrum.
Renee Forsyth, *Memories of Dunoon & Cowal* (Argyll Publishing, 2005).
Tonie and Valmai Holt, *My Boy Jack* (Pen & Sword, 1998).
Another outstanding piece of work by the Holts about the search by Rudyard Kipling for his son's last resting place.
Gordon Irving, *The Good Auld Days* (Jupiter, 1977).

Harry Lauder, *A Minstrel in France* (Andrew Melrose Limited, 1918).

Lorn Macintyre, *Empty Footsteps* (Black Ace Books, 1996).

William Wallace, *Harry Lauder in the Limelight* (The Book Guild, 1988).

Chapter 5

David Harvey, *Monuments to Courage* (Kevin and Kay Patience, 1999).

G. R. Stevens, *A City Goes To War* (Edmonton Regiment Associates, Edmonton, 1963).

Nigel Cave, *Passchendaele: The Fight For The Village* (Pen & Sword, 1997).

F. J. Blatherwick, *1000 Brave Canadians* (Unitrade Press, Toronto, 1991).

Chapter 6

Toni and Valmai Holt, *Violets from Oversea* (Pen & Sword, 1996).

Paul Reed, *Walking the Somme* (Pen & Sword, 1997).

Nigel Cave, *Beaumont-Hamel* (Pen & Sword, 1994).

A.D. Morrison, *History of the 7th Battalion of the Argyll & Sutherland Highlanders* (Printed on behalf of the Battalion in the 1920s, exact date unknown).

Colonel David Rorie, DSO, MD, *A Medico's Luck in the War* (Milne, Aberdeen 1929).

Peter Hart, *Somme Success* (Pen & Sword, 2001).

Tim Skelton and Gerald Gliddon, *Lutyens and the Great War* (Francis Lincoln, 2008).

Gavin Stamp, *The Memorial to the Missing of the Somme* (Profile Books, 2006).

Anthony Babington, *For the Sake of Example* (Pen & Sword, 1993).

Julian Putkowski & Julian Sykes, *Shot at Dawn* (Pen & Sword, 1996).

Leonard Sellars, *For God's Sake Shoot Straight!* (Pen & Sword, 1995).

Chapter 7

Tommy Armour (with Herb Graffis), *How to Play Your Best Golf All the Time* (Simon & Schuster, 1953).

Tommy Armour, *A Round of Golf with Tommy Armour* (Simon & Schuster, 1960).

Christy Campbell, *Band of Brigands* (Harper Press, 2007).

Tom Clavin, *Sir Walter* (Aurum Press, 2005).

E. M. Cockell and Henry Cotton, *The Open at Carnoustie* (*Golf Illustrated*, 12 June, 1931).

Alun Evans, *The Golf Majors* (A & C Black, 2002).

Ross Goodner, *Golf's Greatest* (*Golf Digest*, 1978).

Rich Lerner, *Tommy Armour III* (*Golf Digest*, February, 2009).

Charles J. Smith, *Historic South Edinburgh* (Charles Skilton, 1988).

Charles Price, *The World of Golf* (Cassell, 1963).

Herbert Warren Wind, *The Story of American Golf* (Callaway Editions, 2000).

Chapter 8

Julie Roberts, *Remembering Fromelles* (CWGC, 2010).

Chapter 9

Chaz Bowyer, *Albert Ball VC* (Bridge, 1994).
–, *For Valour: The Air VCs* (Caxton, 2002).
Francis Crosby, *Fighter Aircraft of World Wars I and II* (Southwater, 2010).
Norman Franks & Andy Saunders, *Mannock* (Grub Street, 2008).
Peter Hart, *Aces Falling* (Orion, 2007).
–, *Bloody April* (Cassell, 2005).
–, *Somme Success* (Pen & Sword, 2001).
Jack Herris & Bob Pearson, *Aircraft of World War I* (Amber, 2010).
Cecil Lewis, *Sagittarius Rising* (Penguin, 1983).
Mike O'Connor, *Airfields & Airmen: The Channel Coast* (Pen & Sword, 2005).
–, *Airfields & Airmen: Somme* (Pen & Sword, 2002).
–, *Airfields & Airmen: Ypres* (Pen & Sword, 2001).
Colin Pengelly, *Albert Ball VC* (Pen & Sword, 2010).
W.C.C. Weetman, *The Sherwood Foresters in the Great War* (BiblioBazaar, 2008; Reprint of 1920 original).

Chapter 10

Terence Rattigan, *The Winslow Boy* (Nick Hern Books, 1999 edition).

Chapter 11

Various Authors, *Trails to the Bow: Carseland and Cheadle Chronicles* (University of Calgary, 1980).

Chapter 12

David Harvey, *Monuments to Courage* (Kevin & Kay Patience, 1999).

Chapter 13

Dominiek Dendooven, *The Menin Gate & Last Post* (DeKlaproos, 2005).
Sue Elliott & James Fox, *The Children Who Fought Hitler* (John Murray, 2008).
Dr Gillian Hawkes, *Greater Love Hath No Man: St George's Memorial Church, Ypres* (The Friends of St George's, 2002).
Jacky Platteeuw, *The Great War in Ypres* (Tempus, 2005).
Various Authors, *At the Going Down of the Sun* (Lannoo, 2001).

Chapter 14

Trefor Jones, *On Fame's Eternal Camping Ground* (Self Published, 2007).
Geoff Archer, *The Glorious Dead* (Frontier Publishing, 2009).

David Crane, *Empires of the Dead* (William Collins, 2013).

T.A. Edwin Gibson & G. Kingsley Ward, *Courage Remembered* (HMSO, 1989).

Philip Longworth, *The Unending Vigil* (Leo Cooper/ CWGC, 1985).

Henry Williamson, *The Wet Flanders Plain* (Gliddon Books, 1987).

Ann Clayton, *Chavasse, Double VC* (Pen & Sword, 2003).

Michael Grundy, *A Fiery Glow in the Darkness* (Osborne Heritage, 1997).

3. NEWSPAPERS

Chapter 4

The *Glasgow Herald*
- January 2, 1917: Original report on John Lauder's death.
- May 11, 18, 19, 21, 1976: The Diary Column.
- January 14, 1986: The Diary Column.

The *Sunday Post*
December 5, 1926: Article, 'Looking Back' by Lady Lauder.

The *Daily Record*
October 28, 1977: Article, 'A Story To Touch The Heart'.

Chapter 5

The *Edmonton Journal*
- April 1, 1989: Article by **Bob Gilmour**
- October 3, 2004: Article by **Jim Farrell**

Chapter 7

The *Glasgow Herald*
September 13, 1968: Article by **S.L. McKinlay**.

The *Scotsman*
Various Articles (credited to 'Our Golf Correspondent'):
1921 - 1926 - 1927 - 1928 - 1929 - 1930 - 1931 - 1933 - 1938.

The *Scotsman*
Articles specifically credited:
- **Frank Moran:** August 30, 1963 and October 10, 1968
- **Norman Mair:** December 12, 1977

Scotland On Sunday
Tom English, 'America's Love Affair with the Silver Scot', June 10, 2007.

The *Weekly Record*
Love on the Links, February 5, 1921.

Chapter 9

The *Lenton Listener* (Lenton Community Association Magazine)
Issue #14, September/October, 1981.

The *Nottingham Post*, Article by Andy Smart, May 5, 2017.

Chapter 12

The *Alloa Advertiser*, 1915-16-19.

The *Alloa Journal*, 1915-16.
Plus very important article in issue dated January 27, 1956

Chapter 13

Flanders Today
May 25, 2011, 'De Clerck in talks after amnesty remarks'.

4. DIARIES, LETTERS & ORIGINAL DOCUMENTS

Chapter 4

Personal Diary of Hugh Adam Munro, Lieutenant, 1/8 A&SH, Regimental Museum, Stirling Castle.
The Regimental Diary of the 1/8 A&SH, Regimental Museum, Stirling Castle.
Letter to Mrs E. Lauder Hamilton (Niece of Harry Lauder) from the Ministry of Defence, March 30, 1987.

Chapter 7

REGISTER HOUSE, EDINBURGH:
Marriage Certificate of George and Martha Armour, 1880.
Birth Certificate of Thomas Dickson Armour, 1896.
Death Certificate of George Armour, 1900.
Young versus Armour (Court Proceedings, February 15, 1921).

THE NATIONAL ARCHIVES, LONDON:
1901 Census.
Tommy Armour's Service Record, 1915-1917 (The following years are, I assume, in the 'Burnt Files', since they are not available).
Proceedings of a Medical Board (Army Form A.45), April 2, 1919.
Personal Letter from Tommy Armour to the War Office, December 7, 1918.
Medal Card for Thomas Dickson Armour, December 6, 1918.

Chapter 9

NOTTINGHAMSHIRE ARCHIVES:
The Albert Ball Files, Street Directories etc.

Chapter 12

Programme for play *Lie of the Land* by Gerry Docherty, 2006.
The Canon Lummis File, IWM.
1901 Census.
1911 Census.
McDermond Discharge Papers, The National Archives, London.
McDermond File, Queen's Lancashire Regiment Museum, Fulford Barracks, Preston.
The *London Gazette*, Citations for all four VCs.
Tillicoultry Town Council Minute Book, Entries for December 8, 1915 and December 12, 1915, re: Pollock and Dawson respectively, held at Clackmannanshire Archives.
Royal Observer Corps Association, Article about Pollock, VC by Lawrence Holmes from '10 Group Newsletter'.

5. WEBSITES

Chapter 4

www.sirharrylauder.com
> The most comprehensive Harry Lauder website, administered by James Marturano of New York.

www.jimvallance.com
> This was of great help, especially in the illustration department.

www.electricscotland.com
> Biographical notes on Sir Harry Lauder by Gregory Lauder-Frost (Great Nephew).

www.firstfoot.com

Wikipedia: Jack House.

Chapter 7

American National Biography Online
World Golf Hall of Fame
Wikipedia

Chapter 9

www.albertball.homestead.com
www.cwgc.org
www.lentontimes.co.uk
www.nationalarchives.gov.uk

Chapter 10
Wikipedia entries on *The Winslow Boy*, Terence Rattigan
and George Archer-Shee.
www.edwinjahiel.com
  Movie review by Edwin Jahiel

Chapter 11

Wikipedia entries on Alex Decoteau and Tom Longboat.
www.veterans.gc.ca
  'Native Soldiers, Foreign Battlefields', Veteran Affairs
  Canada, 1996.
www.history.naval.mil
  'Native Americans and the Military' by Roger Bucholz,
  William Fields and Ursula P. Roach.
www.saskatoonlibrary.ca/sports
  Alex Wuttunee Decoteau.
www.biograph.ca
  Alex Decoteau.
www.epl.ca/edmontonacitycalledhome
  Edmonton, A City Called Home: Memories
  N.B. This is THE source on Alex as it contains a
  contribution by Izola Mottershead, his niece, the principal
  authority on the subject.
www.albertasource.ca
  Here, via YouTube, is a very moving short animation
  about Alex.
www.alex-decoteau-run.be
  Information on the Alex Decoteau Run at Passchendaele,
  Belgium.

www.sicc.sk.ca/saskindian

Tom Longboat: A Notable Indian Athlete (Article by Louise Cuthand).

Chapter 12

Wikipedia entries for all four VCs
www.scoop@prestel.co.uk

Grave locations of VCs

6. OTHER MEDIA

Chapter 4

Low Parks Museum, Hamilton: Harry Lauder Exhibition, September 2007-April 2008.

Saltire TV Productions: *Something About Harry*.

Jack House, *Harry Lauder: The Man Who Made The Scotch Comic* (Play presented at The Citizens' Theatre, Glasgow, from May 11 to 17, 1976).

Despite a diligent search through the records of the Mitchell Library and the National Library of Scotland not a trace has been found. It certainly stirred up some fun though!

Chapter 10

The Winslow Boy, Film/DVD, 1999.

Adapted from an original play by Terence Rattigan and directed by David Mamet.

ILLUSTRATION CREDITS

Page 1: Image is in the public domain (IPD).
Page 3: IPD.
Page 10: Image from the author's personal collection (IAPC).
Page 11: IAPC.
Page 12: IAPC.
Page 14: IPD.
Page 15: IAPC.
Page 17: IAPC.
Page 18: IAPC.
Page 20: IAPC.
Page 22: IAPC.
Page 23: IAPC.
Page 25: Image from personal collection of Jim Vallance.
Page 26: IPD.
Page 30: Image from personal collection of Jim Vallance.
Page 32: Image from personal collection of Jim Vallance.
Page 33: IAPC.
Page 37: IAPC.
Page 46: IAPC.
Page 48: Image from personal collection of Jim Vallance.
Page 51: IAPC.
Page 52: Image from personal collection of Jim Vallance.
Page 53: IAPC.
Page 63(a): Image from personal collection of James Marturano.
Page 63(b): Image from personal collection of James Marturano.

Page 65: IPD.

Page 66: IAPC.

Page 69: Image courtesy of Captain Terry Allison, Executive Director, Loyal Edmonton Regiment Military Museum.

Page 70: IAPC.

Page 73: IPD.

Page 77: IAPC.

Page 80: IPD.

Page 81: Image courtesy of Denise & Morris Sigalet, Lougheed, Alberta.

Page 82: Image courtesy of Denise & Morris Sigalet, Lougheed, Alberta.

Page 83: Image courtesy of Denise & Morris Sigalet, Lougheed, Alberta.

Page 91: IAPC.

Page 94: IAPC.

Page 96: IAPC.

Page 99: IAPC.

Page 100: IPD.

Page 101: IAPC.

Page 105: IAPC.

Page 106: IAPC.

Page 107: IAPC.

Page 108: IAPC.

Page 109: IAPC.

Page 112: IAPC.

Page 113: IAPC.

Page 114: IAPC.

Page 118: IPD.

Page 119: IAPC.

Page 120: IAPC.

Page 124(a): Image courtesy of Major Colin Hepburn,
Regimental Secretary, Royal Tank Regiment.
Page 124(b): Image courtesy of Major Colin Hepburn,
Regimental Secretary, Royal Tank Regiment.
Page 130: IPD.
Page 143: IPD.
Page 149: IPD.
Page 152: IAPC.
Page 153: IAPC.
Page 156: IAPC.
Page 157: IAPC.
Page 158(a): IAPC.
Page 158(b): IAPC.
Page 159: IAPC.
Page 160: IAPC.
Page 162: IAPC.
Page 165: IPD.
Page 166: IAPC.
Page 167: IAPC.
Page 170: IAPC.
Page 174: IPD.
Page 175: IPD.
Page 177: IPD.
Page 181: IPD.
Page 182: IPD.
Page 186: IAPC.
Page 187: IAPC.
Page 188: IAPC.
Page 189(a): IAPC.
Page 189(b): IAPC.
Page 190: IAPC.
Page 196: IAPC.

Page 200: IPD.

Page 202: IAPC.

Page 203: IAPC.

Page 204: IPD.

Page 205: IPD.

Page 206: IPD.

Page 207: Image courtesy of the Government of Ontario.

Page 212: IPD.

Page 216(a): IPD.

Page 216(b): IAPC.

Page 217: IPD.

Page 221: Image courtesy of Royal Engineers Library, Chatham.

Page 226: IPD.

Page 230: IAPC.

Page 232(a): Image courtesy of Clackmannan County Council.

Page 232(b): IAPC.

Page 234: IAPC.

Page 235: IAPC.

Page 237: IAPC.

Page 238: IAPC.

Page 239(a): IAPC.

Page 239(b): IAPC.

Page 240: IAPC.

Page 241(a): IAPC.

Page 241(b): IAPC.

Page 242: IAPC.

Page 243(a): IAPC.

Page 243(b): IAPC.

Page 244: IAPC.

Page 245: IAPC.

Page 246: IAPC.
Page 248: IAPC.
Page 249: IPD.
Page 250: IAPC.
Page 254: IAPC.
Page 255(a): IAPC.
Page 255(b): IPD.
Page 256: IAPC.
Page 257: IAPC.
Page 260: IPD.
Page 262: IAPC.
Page 263: IPD.
Page 264: IAPC.
Page 265: IAPC.
Page 266: IPD.

About the Author

I was born in late 1938 in the small town of Tillicoultry at the foot of the Ochil Hills in Central Scotland and was educated locally and at the University of Edinburgh. On first leaving secondary school I worked for three years as an apprentice mining surveyor during which time I was stationed at various collieries in the local coalfield. Despite enjoying my spell in the coal industry in the company of the fine lads in the survey department and the miners underground, it became clear that a surveyor's life was not for me due to my inability to grasp the intricacies of the theodolite and its attendant maths. So it was with a sigh of relief on the part of all concerned that I left an honest job and set off on the path to becoming a teacher of history.

On completing an MA degree at Edinburgh in 1963 I went off to America for four months. I toured around on a go-anywhere bus ticket covering a lot of the ground east of the Mississippi including quite a while in the South which certainly opened my eyes to some basic human truths. Remember this was 1963! Returning to Scotland I took an educational qualification and after three years of teaching English and History in a local secondary school I went back to the University of Edinburgh to study for a postgraduate degree in North American studies, an almost inevitable choice given the influence of my Stateside peregrinations.

After graduation I was employed for three years in adult education in my home area before returning to secondary school teaching where I remained until retiral in 1999. During my time in the classroom I was successively head of History in three local schools, culminating in a 21-year tenure at Grangemouth High School on the south shore of the River Forth. Although teaching can have its stressful moments I have never regretted spending the majority of my life in the classroom. The number of genuinely nice people I met during this time, both pupils and staff, and the number of laughs I had far outweighed those down times that occur in any job. On a personal level, the most important results of my time in education were meeting my wife Janey, a PE teacher, and visiting the battlefields of both World Wars with the pupils. Beginning in 1981, these battlefield excursions became annual events with the result that I've now been over to Flanders and France thirty-one times.

I began researching and writing about WWI in 2005, having been requested by a local politician to find out about the four Victoria Cross holders from our home county, Clackmannanshire. Then, I suppose, to paraphrase the old cliché, "it just growed". Since then I have produced a website, a Kindle book, and delivered lectures on various WWI-related personalities including, of course, Harry Lauder. My interest in Harry was initially sparked by correspondence in the *Glasgow Herald*, a major Scottish newspaper, about his son's demise and things took off from there. My fascination for the Great War has never diminished, indeed it increases as more and more information becomes available in these centenary years. Though I'm now pushing along, another trip or two is not out of the question.

Also Available from Extremis Publishing

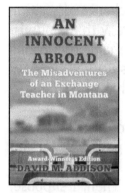

An Innocent Abroad

The Misadventures of an Exchange Teacher in Montana

By David M. Addison

When, in 1978, taking a bold step into the unknown, the author, accompanied by his wife and young family, swapped his boring existence in Grangemouth in central Scotland for life in Missoula, Montana, in the western United States, he could never have foreseen just how much of a life-changing experience it would turn out to be.

As an exchange teacher, he was prepared for a less formal atmosphere in the classroom, while, for their part, his students had been warned that he would be "Mr Strict". It was not long before this clash of cultures reared its ugly head and the author found life far more "exciting" than he had bargained for. Within a matter of days of taking up his post, he found himself harangued in public by an irate parent, while another reported him to the principal for "corrupting" young minds.

Outwith the classroom, he found daily life just as shocking. Lulled by a common language into a false sense of a "lack of foreignness", he was totally unprepared for the series of culture shocks that awaited him from the moment he stepped into his home for the year – the house from *Psycho*.

There were times when he wished he had stayed at home in his boring but safe existence in Scotland, but mainly this is a heart-warming and humorous tale of how this Innocent abroad, reeling from one surprising event to the next, gradually begins to adapt to his new life. And thanks to a whole array of colourful personalities and kind people (hostile parents not withstanding), he finally comes to realise that this exchange was the best thing he had ever done.

The Spectrum of Adventure

A Brief History of Interactive Fiction on the Sinclair ZX Spectrum

By Thomas A. Christie

The Sinclair ZX Spectrum was one of the most popular home computers in British history, selling over five million units in its 1980s heyday. Amongst the thousands of games released for the Spectrum during its lifetime, the text adventure game was to emerge as one of the most significant genres on the system.

The Spectrum of Adventure chronicles the evolution of the text adventure on the ZX Spectrum, exploring the work of landmark software houses such as Melbourne House Software, Level 9 Computing, Delta 4 Software, the CRL Group, Magnetic Scrolls, and many others besides.

Covering one hundred individual games in all, this book celebrates the Spectrum's thriving interactive fiction scene of the eighties, chronicling the achievements of major publishers as well as independent developers from the machine's launch in 1982 until the end of the decade in 1989.

A Righteously Awesome Eighties Christmas
Festive Cinema of the 1980s

By Thomas A. Christie

The cinema of the festive season has blazed a trail through the world of film-making for more than a century, ranging from silent movies to the latest CGI features. From the author of *The Christmas Movie Book*, this new text explores the different narrative themes which emerged in the genre over the course of the 1980s, considering the developments which have helped to make the Christmas films of that decade amongst the most fascinating and engaging motion pictures in the history of festive movie production.

Released against the backdrop of a turbulent and rapidly-changing world, the Christmas films of the 1980s celebrated traditions and challenged assumptions in equal measure. With warm nostalgia colliding with aggressive modernity as never before, the eighties saw the movies of the holiday season being deconstructed and reconfigured to remain relevant in an age of cynicism and innovation.

Whether exploring comedy, drama, horror or fantasy, Christmas cinema has an unparalleled capacity to attract and inspire audiences. With a discussion ranging from the best-known titles to some of the most obscure, *A Righteously Awesome Eighties Christmas* examines the ways in which the Christmas motion pictures of the 1980s fit into the wider context of this captivating and ever-evolving genre.

Planes on Film
Ten Favourite Aviation Films

By Colin M. Barron

One of the most durable genres in cinema, the aviation film has captivated audiences for decades with tales of heroism, bravery and overcoming seemingly insurmountable odds. Some of these movies have become national icons, achieving critical and commercial success when first released in cinemas and still attracting new audiences today.

In *Planes on Film: Ten Favourite Aviation Films*, Colin M. Barron reveals many little-known facts about the making of several aviation epics. Every movie is discussed in comprehensive detail, including a thorough analysis of the action and a complete listing of all the aircraft involved. With information about where the various planes were obtained from and their current location, the book also explores the subject of aviation films which were proposed but ultimately never saw the light of day.

With illustrations and meticulous factual commentary, *Planes on Film* is a book which will appeal to aviation enthusiasts, military historians and anyone who has an interest in cinema. Written by an author with a lifelong passion for aircraft and their depiction on the silver screen, *Planes on Film* presents a lively and thought-provoking discourse on a carefully-chosen selection of movies which have been drawn from right across the history of this fascinating cinematic genre.

Dying Harder
Action Movies of the 1980s

By Colin M. Barron

The 1980s were a golden age for action movies, with the genre proving popular at the box-office as never before. Across the world, stars such as Sylvester Stallone, Arnold Schwarzenegger and Bruce Willis were becoming household names as a result of their appearances in some of the best-known films of the decade.

But what were the stories which lay behind the making of these movies? Why were the eighties to bear witness to so many truly iconic action features? And who were the people who brought these legends of action cinema to life?

In *Dying Harder: Action Movies of the 1980s*, Colin M. Barron considers some of the most unforgettable movies of the decade, exploring the reasons behind their success and assessing the extent of their enduring acclaim amongst audiences which continues into the present day.

For details of new and forthcoming books
from Extremis Publishing,
please visit our official website at:

www.extremispublishing.com

or follow us on social media at:

www.facebook.com/extremispublishing

www.linkedin.com/company/extremis-publishing-ltd-/

Lightning Source UK Ltd.
Milton Keynes UK
UKHW02f1837221117
313134UK00006B/402/P